AMAZING
yoga

AMAZING yoga

A Practical Guide to Strength, Wellness, and Spirit

Sean and Karen Conley

Westwood Books
PITTSBURGH

Copyright ©2010 by Sean Conley and Karen Conley

Cover photo by Duane Rieder
Yoga photos by Kelley Bedoloto
Design by Kathy Boykowycz

All rights reserved. No part of this book may be reproduced in any form whatsoever without written permission from the copyright holders, except in the case of brief quotations embodied in critical reviews or essays. For information contact Autumn House Press, 87½ Westwood Street, Pittsburgh PA 15211.

"Autumn House" and "Autumn House Press" are registered trademarks owned by Autumn House Press, a nonprofit corporation whose mission is the publication and promotion of poetry and other fine literature. Westwood Books is an imprint of Autumn House Press.

Autumn House Press Staff
Editor-in-Chief and Founder: Michael Simms
Executive Director: Richard St. John
Community Outreach Director: Michael Wurster
Co-Founder: Eva-Maria Simms
Fiction Editor: Sharon Dilworth
Associate Editor: Ziggy Edwards
Assistant Editors: Evan Oare, Kriscinda Meadows
Media Consultant: Jan Beatty
Publishing Consultant: Peter Oresick
Tech Crew Chief: Michael Milberger
Intern: Athena Pappas

This project was supported by the Pennsylvania Council on the Arts, a state agency, through its regional arts funding partnership, Pennsylvania Partners in the Arts (PPA). State government funding comes through an annual appropriation by Pennsylvania's General Assembly. PPA is administered in Allegheny County by Greater Pittsburgh Arts Council.

ISBN: 978-1-932870-42-8

Library of Congress: 2010933676

All Autumn House books are printed on acid-free paper and meet the international standards of permanent books intended for purchase by libraries.

Acknowledgments

We would like to thank all of the people who helped make this book possible.

Sharon Dilworth, without you this book would have never happened. We thank you for your encouragement and for influencing the genesis of this book from the first day at the coffee shop.

To Jen Lee, thank you for your encouragement and the many hours you spent pouring your heart into this book. A special thanks to one heck of a photographer, Duane Reider. Thank you for getting up in the middle of the night with your crew to work. The Pittsburgh sunrise was fabulous!

To Kelley Bedoloto, thank you for your enthusiastic and magical work photographing the poses. Thank you to Joy Sakonyi, for sharing your expertise in Naturopathy.

Thanks to our first yoga teacher, Baron Baptiste. Thank you for providing us with the inspiration to teach yoga!

Thank you to all the students who have come to our studios and teacher trainings. And thank you to all the students who shared themselves and their stories for this book. We are eternally grateful to you. Thanks to all the teachers and managers at Amazing Yoga for your support, enthusiasm, and passion.

Thanks to our parents, who have put up with us for almost 40 years now. Thank you for your love and support. Thanks to our greatest joy in the world, our kids: Sadie, Summer, Scout, and Jack. We love you!

Contents

PREFACE

How We Found Yoga, *or*
How Yoga Found Us   3

PART ONE

Yoga: It's Simple and
Practical, Yet Powerful   13

PART TWO

Eight Guiding Intentions
for Your Yoga Practice   21

PART THREE

On Your Mat:
Power Vinyasa
Yoga Sequences   93

PART FOUR

Mindful Eating   133

PART FIVE

Making Everything
in Your Life Yoga   143

Preface

How We
Found Yoga
or
How Yoga
Found Us

AMAZING
yoga

How Sean Found Yoga / How Yoga Found Sean

There is a Buddhist proverb that says, "When the student is ready, the teacher will appear." The "teachers" are not necessarily people but in fact events or experiences in your life. You may have one of those "*aha*" moments, a light bulb going off, or you may learn gradually, through a series of experiences. The key is being open, ready to learn, because the arrival of our teacher isn't really about someone or something coming into our lives; it's about what happens inside of us. In fact, our teacher may have been hanging around for a while, we just didn't notice. Then one day, we do. My teachers were injuries, the loss of a loved one, and the birth of my first child. Finally, I got the hint and woke up to my own life.

Yoga is a journey, not a destination. The pleasure of the practice is in getting there, not in achieving—kind of like life. In the same way, the path of discovering yoga and making it an integral part of your life is different for everyone. Mine started when I was in college—playing football at the University of Pittsburgh. During my career, I developed hip and lower back injuries so painful that I had to crawl on hands and knees to make it to the bathroom. The back spasms came out of nowhere; simply changing the dial on the car radio would set my lower back off and I would be in excruciating pain. It was so intense that the only way I could play football was by taking muscle relaxants.

With encouragement from Karen, I started doing yoga to help ease my physical pain. At the time I was living near the university where my roommate was a strange, original cook. He would cobble together odd dishes like eggs and pierogies, topping them off with hot sauce and cottage cheese. He'd eat some of it then disappear, leaving his half-finished culinary masterpiece on the living room floor. That's where I first did yoga—in that apartment between a beat-up

As a Detroit Lion, getting in a lunge pose in before a game with the Cincinnati Bengals

Our marriage day at the Broward County Courthouse in Fort Lauderdale with Judge Larry Seidlin

couch, a rummage sale TV and plates of moldy pierogies and eggs.

My first National Football League gig was with the Detroit Lions in 1993. After a summer of intense training in Pittsburgh, I left for Pontiac, Michigan where the Lions had their training camp. Scraping pennies, Karen would visit me in her beautiful metallic orange Ford Firenza, complete with shiny bald tires. I did well in training camp, but in the end they made the choice to stick with their veteran kicker.

Released from Detroit, I decided to move to a warmer climate where I could train in the winter months. Karen and I found an apartment in Coral Springs, Florida, where I took a job as the bellman at the Pompano Beach Resort. It was the coolest place for a 24-year-old guy like me to work. The New York Yankees stayed there during spring training, and one of my duties was to deliver George Steinbrenner's dry cleaning. I got to see the owner of the Yankees in his underwear. Steinbrenner would give me five bucks and say, "Thanks kid." Very cool. Frank Sinatra also stayed there, and I became an "honorary bodyguard" for Ol' Blue Eyes.

In Florida, I was doing a little yoga but was still not completely sold on what it could do for me. One thing that I was sold on was Karen, and it was there that we tied the knot. My agent had a fun, spirited brother who was a judge—Judge Seidlin (who would later gain notoriety in the Anna Nicole Smith case). Our wedding was in the Broward County Courthouse and the witness was Judge Seidlin's secretary (who had to be interrupted as she was in the middle of giving herself a makeover with nail polish and makeup). Halfway through the short ceremony, the judge asked Karen why she was marrying a loser like me when she could drive to South Beach with him in his cool red convertible. Lucky for me, Karen declined the judge's offer, and we were married. We left right away for our honeymoon in Key West, but ran out of money in Key Largo. Someone was looking out for us though—it was Arby's. Five roast beef sandwiches for five bucks. Wedded bliss.

As the off-season came to a close, I was running out of time to find a spot on a roster. Luckily, my agent lined up a one-day workout with the Miami Dolphins. The day started out well: my kicks cleared the fence behind the goal posts, and some of them even hit the side of a white van parked in the lot beyond. After it happened a few times, I asked if we should back up, but the coach didn't seem to think it was a big deal. "I know who owns that van. He won't mind," he said. A couple more van hits and Hall of Fame quarterback Dan Marino walked onto the field. "Sign that kid up right now," he shouted to us. "His aim is right on. He's hit my van enough times." The Dolphins didn't sign me—Dan must not have had much pull with the team higher-ups. Go figure.

Soon after, I signed with the Indianapolis Colts and resumed my usual intense training (or overtraining) during the summer before training camp. Three weeks into camp my leg gave out, and the team released me.

I went back to Pittsburgh and got a job driving a truck for UPS and picked up one of my other "in-between football gigs" delivering food. Still, I was so determined to make it in the NFL that I thought about turning up at the Steelers facility to deliver a package and showing them my kicking skills, all the while dressed in brown. I also worked for a couple of weeks driving an ice cream truck, but listening to "It's A Small World After All" over and over, all day long, was putting me over the edge.

Sean on the sidelines with the Indianapolis Colts in 1995 before a game against the Seattle Seahawks

Then, in the spring of 1995, I got a call from the NY Jets to come up for a tryout. It was incredible, a dream job! Karen had graduated from Fordham in the Bronx, so she was equally excited. Pumped on adrenaline, I had a great workout, connecting on multiple field goals from beyond 60 yards. I signed a two-year contract with the Jets and would report back in July for training camp to compete for the job. The situation looked bright. They had an aging kicker who was winding down his career; I was just 25 and had a strong leg again. Before the fall training camp, they sent me to Scotland to play in a newly created developmental league, and the extra work on my leg proved to be too much.

When I returned to the Jets, their physician said that both of my hip flexors had degenerated. At the time I didn't know what that meant, but I knew it wasn't good. Any word with *de-* in front of it usually isn't. The writing was on the wall.

Still, I decided to give it one more shot. My dad was a huge supporter of my football quest, and I had an opportunity to play in the Canadian Football League, so we drove together to Birmingham. At the time, my dad was battling colon cancer and was taking an experimental drug that had to be delivered via syringe and kept in a cooler. We did a lot of talking on that trip, about football, life, and kids. I had terrible allergies and sneezed the entire drive back to Pittsburgh. I went through two boxes of tissues and it drove him nuts.

But it was during that trip that what mattered most in my life became clear. Instead of beating up my body, focusing on making money and accomplishing my NFL dream, I knew it was time to live a more balanced life. One that focused on my family, my kids, and celebrating the joys of life. That was the end. I knew it was time to move on.

That's when Karen and I decided that we were going to change our livelihoods. Yoga was going to be a central part of our lives. One of our studios, in a neighborhood called Shadyside, is near the University of Pittsburgh. It's not far from my old North Oakland apartment, the one where I first did yoga—the one with the messy roommate and the beat-up old couch. Sometimes, I drive by that apartment and wonder if anyone has picked up that plate of pierogies yet.

How Karen Found Yoga / How Yoga Found Karen

After 12 years of teaching yoga and living my own yoga experience, I have come to believe that yoga finds us just at the moment when we need it most. Here is how yoga found me:

A recent college graduate, I had moved home to Erie, Pennsylvania, and was expecting my first child. Exercise was limited—weather and opportunity, financial constraints. I was also experiencing a series of drastic lifestyle changes—the baby, Sean, living back in the town where I had grown up—my post-college life was not exactly as I had planned it during my years of intense undergraduate studies.

My mother, oddly enough, had a collection of yoga videos. I tried them out and they made me feel better. There was no intense change, but the practice provided some relief from the angst I was feeling.

Then, my baby was born. As a first-time mother, I didn't understand how my daily schedule would be turned upside down. There was no time for yoga. A few years passed and I had another baby, my second adorable girl, and I was less shellshocked by the changes in my life. Back up at my mother's place, I found a brochure for Kripalu, a yoga retreat center in western Massachusetts. I read about a weekend retreat for something called Power Yoga. I liked how it was described—it reminded me of the classes I had taught in aerobics and kickboxing years ago. So I decided to go. My mother said she'd come along.

To avoid driving through the unpredictable winters of the Northeast, particularly the lake-effect snow those of us who grew up near the Great Lakes know so well, my mother decided we would take a train. She thought it sounded adventurous—something women explorers would do at the drop of a hat. Because of my two babies, I only had so much time away and did not want to rely on a train, but she had already deter-

> We do not receive wisdom. We must discover it for ourselves after a journey through the wilderness, which no one can make for us, which no one can spare us, for our wisdom is the point of view from which we come at last to regard the world.
>
> **MARCEL PROUST**

mined that it was the safest way to travel and it did make sense. Part of me was impatient with the idea of a 12-hour train ride to the Berkshires because I would not be in control. But there was no arguing with Mom, and I had to let it go.

The trip took longer than expected and we arrived at our destination late. No one was there to meet us. Nothing at our stop but an empty plastic-covered cove and an empty bench. We had luggage, it was snowing, and the temperature was raw. A friendly local rescued us and took us all the way to the yoga retreat, teaching me that, like yoga, the universe sometimes takes care of us just when we need it most.

The yoga center at Kripalu is very simple, very unstressful. It helped me relax after the trip and gave me hope that things might turn out all right.

I walked into the first workshop ready, but I was immediately intimidated. The room was full of people—there were at least 200 students getting their gear ready—and everyone else seemed very comfortable. I was new to yoga, new to this scene, and not at all sure about any of it.

Class started.

It was challenging but inspiring—a combination that astonished me. After class, I went to my room to write in my journal. Something had changed within. The workshop seemed to be speaking directly to me, and I knew I was in the right place. The classes struck a deep chord in my body: my thoughts were clear, my body felt good. I was in my twenties and wondered why I hadn't always felt that way. The exercise part was not new to me—that felt natural; it was the clarity of mind that made the difference. I knew I was ready to be more involved in my life, tired of just going through the motions. I knew I wanted something different, that I felt on the edge of a precipice. I didn't know what was out there, but now I knew it was there.

I finished the weekend in a resting pose called Savasana and felt my jaw release and my body relax in a way it hadn't in a long time, if ever. Now I would call that feeling peacefulness, calmness—I wasn't worrying about my life, even the next task. It was clear to me that this practice worked out the stress in a way that would enable me to re-enter the intensity of my life, without letting myself be so intense. I signed up for a teacher training in Mexico; teaching had been my profession before having kids, so it seemed like a natural path. I wanted to share the freshness and power of this ancient practice with others.

I was ready.

After my first training in Mexico with Baron Baptiste, I came back and started honing my skills as a teacher. The studios in Pittsburgh were limited, and one day while Sean and I were driving to the grocery store we passed an empty retail space.

"That looks like a great yoga studio," I said.

"Let's do it," Sean replied.

I was unsure, but Sean called the real estate agent and two days later we signed a lease, a total leap of faith. Our neighbors designed the website and logo. Sean installed the floor and painted the walls. Four weeks later, we opened for business. We had a party and invited all of our friends. We were so excited.

Monday morning came and the first class began at 9:30. I sat patiently, getting nervous as the minutes passed. The teacher was there, but no one showed. I called Sean at 9:45 and started to cry. New beginnings are not always easy, my practice had taught me that. The first week of the opening was quiet—fewer than 50 students came through the door. But we were not in a rush—yoga had taught us the importance of process. Eventually word got around, and soon 500 people were coming each week. A few years later and 1,000 students would show up each week to take our classes.

What has surprised us is that even in the midst of a difficult economic climate, more and more people are taking up yoga. In 2009, millions of new students started going to yoga for the first time. People are finding yoga to be therapeutic in so many ways—for body, mind and soul. The old fitness mindset of beating up our bodies and pushing ourselves to the limit is waning. Yoga allows people to take care of themselves. It allows us to gain strength internally and externally so that we can give to others.

The practice of yoga has shaped my entire life. It has allowed me to be more present and aware of what I do and how I do it. This doesn't mean that I am always calm, present or peaceful, but it reminds me that that's how I want to be. Yoga has put me on a path to enjoy each day as something special. In the past few years, it has meant looking forward to a new morning and a cup of hot coffee, which I now take the time to taste and enjoy as I prepare for the day about to begin. Four kids, a husband, an energetic Lab, and four yoga studios—the day swirls together quickly.

I have learned that being honest with people is usually best even though it is the most challenging. I practice this way of living with my children and in turn they have practiced it with me. The work I do in my life is not limited by the boundaries of seeking perfection. Instead, I am always working to be a kinder, more accepting and loving person.

This path always has room for growth.

One

Yoga:
It's Simple
and Practical,
Yet Powerful

AMAZING yoga

When we were looking to open our first studio back in 2001, yoga was in its infancy in Pittsburgh. People were curious—they'd heard the buzz about yoga. Celebrities were jumping on the yoga bandwagon: Madonna was doing down dogs, Christy Turlington was gracing the cover of *Time* in lotus pose, and Sting was busting out Warrior 1 poses on Trans-Atlantic flights. For us, it was always, "You've got to try yoga—it's amazing!" But people wanted more. They wanted to know why. Why was it amazing? What was so great about it? When people hear the word yoga, they often think: pretzel poses, skinny people, gentle stretching, weird chanting, maybe even an eye pillow thrown in the mix. Perhaps this is why so many of us must literally be dragged to our first class. Then, we find ourselves trying to convince a friend to try yoga. But it's a tough sell, maybe because it's so hard to put the experience into words.

Back then, we responded with elaborate reasons for trying yoga, listing the benefits of the practice. But we always came back to simply urging people to try. "You've got to do it," we insisted. "You will feel amazing when you do." Amazing describes how we feel about our yoga, and so our name was born:

Karen: I think we should call our studio *Amazing Yoga*.
Sean: How about *Incredible Yoga*?
Karen: It makes me think of the Incredible Hulk.
Sean: *Phenomenal Yoga*?
Karen: Too many syllables.
Sean: How about *Marvelous Yoga*?
Karen: Nobody uses that word anymore!
Sean: OK, then. How about *Awesome Yoga*?
Karen: No, that's over-hyping it. It's *Amazing*. Case closed.

---

amazing

definition:
· Something that is so wonderful, it is hard to find words to describe it
· Something that happens in the extraordinary
· Something that is rare and brings an unexpected kick into your life

yoga

definition:
To connect or bring together

amazing +yoga

· Bring together that which is so wonderful it's hard to put into words
· Bring together something that happens in the extraordinary
· Bring together something that is rare and brings an unexpected kick into your life

According to a study by Yoga Journal, in 2008 over 18 million Americans were practicing yoga. In 2009, nine million more were expected to take up the practice. Why are so many people turning to yoga?

Here's why: Yoga can make you to feel amazing! Add yoga to your life and soon your attitude and outlook will change. You discover that the joy woven into your life has been there all along. As your body and mind awaken, your personal awareness heightens. Your body teaches you to listen. You relate to yourself and others in a new way, and this mindfulness is the key. The toned abs and chiseled butt cheeks are nice, but they are just by-products of this incredible practice.

Yoga teaches us that we are already perfect. We posses such wisdom, yet we walk through life asleep to what we know. By revealing that we set our own limitations, yoga wakes us up. The mind is a wonderful storyteller. Each day it creates a fictional world that fools us away from the joy and harmony that are already part of our lives. If we let it, the mind can keep us from becoming boundless. Most of us don't achieve anywhere close to our full potential. Yet, as we practice yoga, we decide that we would rather be happy and our limitations fall away. Why show up in your life as a 3 when you can be a 10? It's our choice.

Yoga is quite simple, yet it possesses an incredible vastness—it is immense and practical at the same time. Over time, you will discover the seamlessness of yoga. Everything becomes yoga. You take what you learn on your mat—to be more forgiving, more gentle, less judgmental—and apply it to the outside world. Sometimes this is a challenge, and sometimes it is effortless. On our mats, we can face our fears in a safe environment.

We all know that we have little control over the external facts of our lives. Yet we have control over what goes on inside, how we react. Many of us are busier than ever these days, addicted to distractions, bored if we are not doing "something." Yoga offers the chance to find a little peace and quiet. For 90 minutes there is no email, no Facebook, no TV, no cell phone, no newspaper, no laundry or dishes to do. You are just practicing, being alive, and being present.

Yoga is a celebration of life.

Simply put, yoga works. It's been around for more than 5,000 years. Putting your trust in yoga is putting faith in a practice that has a proven track record for strengthening and healing. If you are still not convinced, that's ok. But before you try to come up with an excuse to get out of trying yoga, let's see if we got it covered:

Excuses   Great News!

Excuses	Great News!
I'm not flexible.	Yoga improves flexibility.
I'm not very good at it.	Just do your best! It's not a competition.
I'm out of shape.	Yoga will get you in the best shape of your life.
I need my cardio.	Yoga works your heart and lungs.
I'm stressed out.	Yoga will help you manage stress.
I don't have the time.	Just 20 minutes a day will do.
Yoga is just for girls.	Men do yoga: Dan Marino, Shaq, The Pittsburgh Steelers, forklift operators, and many more tough guys

Don't worry about not getting a strong "workout." In yoga, the workout is part of the deal. Yoga will strengthen your body like you have never imagined. And yes, if you practice regularly, you will experience physical benefits like losing weight and toning muscles. Don't worry about yoga being "new-agey" either. Yoga is too old for that. You don't have to go to India to learn more about it either. All the yoga you need is right here. You just have to get on your mat and do it. But here's the best part—you will soon discover that you can practice yoga everywhere you go:

Karen working with Pittsburgh Steeler Tight End Matt Spaeth

at your job   in the Target parking lot
in line at Disney World   in rush hour traffic
in line at the post office in all your relationships

The powers of yoga are astounding. Through yoga, we are able to create high levels of energy, happiness, joy, and peace. Yoga gives us the place to work within ourselves and away from fighting our minds and egos. Yoga is not easy; it is actually quite challenging. However, over time, we learn how to find a balance between working hard and being sensitive to our bodies. Yoga is not about going beyond your limits. We begin to treat our bodies gently and we nuture them and honor them, and this promotes healing.

These days many of us feel the constant need to compare ourselves with others. We turn almost everything we do into some sort of competition. In yoga, there are no competitions, no grading scales, no performance plans. Once we are able to get to a place where we no longer compare ourselves with others and become committed to true health, we can make dramatic changes in our lives. It's moving to a place of giving ourselves what we need instead of what we want.

Why would we want to devote so much time comparing ourselves with others? Each one of us is so different and unique in so many ways. In yoga, we are striving towards true health and wellness, which does not consist of comparing and contrasting your body to those around you. We are all meant to be unique.

We look at our yoga practice like a compass: it helps lead us in the right direction. We may go off-course from time to time, but we just right the ship again. We focus on being happy in that moment, not once we have achieved a certain something. We all know about getting caught up in the wheel of always wanting and never being truly happy with where we're at. To find happiness, we must look within, and yoga teaches us how to do that. We will not find it outside of ourselves. We must practice living in the now. Yoga brings us into the moment. We become less reactive to things that are out of our control. We become comfortable in uncomfortable places.

Yoga will awaken your entire body. Every square inch will be touched. It reinvigorates your mind. It's a safe environment to work on what you need to work on. All the negative aspects of your life are exposed(jealousy, greed, or simply put, wanting). Yoga will quiet your mind and help you eradicate negative thoughts. We practice patience and forgiveness in yoga. Then we take the next step and take it out the door with us. Once our mind begins to heal, the body will heal in step. It will take an open mind, a big mind for this to happen. As we know, our minds have no boundaries. We end up in a place of balance, of harmony, of joy, and of connection with nature and to the people around us. This is how we discover our true power. This personal power is being ourselves, standing on our own two feet.

We have seen it work for countless people, which is why we want to share our love of yoga and spread it around. Yoga is a wisdom that everyone experiences individually. This is why we have included personal stories from a variety of yoga practitioners in the book. Students who practice yoga can explain their feelings and experiences better than anyone else. But don't take their word for it. Pick and choose the parts of the book that resonate with you. Then, try it yourself. Experience it for yourself!

Two

Eight Guiding Intentions for Your Yoga Practice

AMAZING yoga

Intention:

· an aim that guides action

· a purpose or attitude toward the effect of one's actions or conduct

· a determination to act in a certain way

WHAT IS YOUR INTENTION?

What are you hoping to create? What are you looking to get rid of? Why do you practice yoga? Yoga is a unique experience for everyone. Each one of us can find something in it that will resonate with our hearts and minds. Each time you come onto your yoga mat, you can have a completely different experience than the last time. Whatever is happening currently in your life affects your practice. If you're holding onto anger, resentment, fear, anxiety, yoga gives you the opportunity to let go. This practice is profound, it is powerful, and it can be life changing. For yoga to work, bring an open mind to your mat. Breathe, breathe, breathe. Life is a journey, not a destination. Let's enjoy the ride.

Setting an intention is not focusing on a future outcome. Intention is "your reason," why you practice yoga. It allows you to think about what you are looking to create on your mat. Intention is a practice or path that is completely focused on how you are "being" in the present moment. While experiencing the ever-changing flow of life, your attention is solely on the always present "now." You choose an intention based on what matters most to you. You follow up intention with focus and, most importantly, commitment—a commitment to match your actions with your inner wisdom and spirit.

You will begin to experience a release. Remember that feeling. What might seem like problems may actually be invitations for change. Yoga is a state of mind. Our hope is that we maintain the yoga throughout our everyday living. The poses and movements in yoga mimic life. The poses and movements are opportunities or experiences for us to practice living. You attempt to maintain calmness and focus throughout. By not reacting to the challenging moments, you lessen the power of your weaknesses. This allows you to strengthen yourself physically, emotionally and spiritually.

Setting an intention for your practice will put your positive thoughts into action. These actions and intentions result in phenomenal power! We practice focusing which allows us to be present. We practice breathing which makes us calm.

When we set an intention, we are practicing living in the present moment. This is quite different from setting goals that focus on future outcomes such as a job promotion, finding a spouse, etc. This makes yoga and intentions special. Look at setting an intention as something you "practice." Yoga is a place to be, not a place to get. We are fully aware of every moment. Your intention is of deep importance to you and you follow through with the highest level of commitment. You match what you know to be true with your actions in life.

Yoga does not have an On/Off button. You cannot just turn it on and become instantly forgiving. These intentions stay with you daily. But being aware of what you need to work on is the first crucial step.

By constantly remaining focused on our true intentions, it will allow us to live a fuller, freer life, one that is not attached to wanting, achievements, doubts, and insecurities.

This will enable us to live a life in harmony and balance, one that is focused on making other people happy instead of ourselves. The greatest gift is giving: our love, our time, and a part of ourselves.

Of course life will present us with its ups and downs. But by staying grounded with your intentions, you will be able to move with the flow. This commitment to being who you are and being comfortable in your

> We make a living by what we get, but we make a life by what we give.
>
> **WINSTON CHURCHILL**

own skin keeps you from the obsession of wanting and achieving. This will not keep you immune to pain and fear, but you will have a way of staying strong through it all. It will keep you in command of your happiness and being joyful regardless of the external events.

Try to not judge yourself as you work through the process. Stay focused on being present. Awareness is the first step toward moving to positive results.

For example, if you go to yoga and you are already consumed with thoughts of vanity (I wish my ass was smaller, I wish I had more money, I wish I was flexible like her), try not to focus on these things, or you will end up with negative results. You will just end up being more obsessed with these things.

If you go to yoga and focus your intention on positive thoughts (i.e., not wanting, and gratitude) you will begin to free yourself of self-limiting thoughts. By staying grounded in intention, we now have control over how we react to events and circumstances in life. This is mindfulness.

HOW DO WE KNOW IF OUR INTENTIONS ARE COMING FROM THE RIGHT PLACE?

We must move toward what is called "the heart center." This is our inner wisdom or our awakened inner mind-heart that we must rely on.

By living a life filled with intention, you stay anchored to loving and giving to others. It gives you the strength to resist falling for ego, vanity and materialism. Yoga is confrontational: we must commit and work on what we know we need to work on. By practicing and practicing, these intentions will eventually become your way of life. By giving it attention it will thrive and grow.

Keep trying to connect with this inner wisdom. Let go of the thought that it will be easy. You may fall off the path, just get back on. By continually coming back to your intention you move towards freedom and your own true self. Keep coming back to your heart center.

If you are struggling in a certain pose, it's ok. You can work on giving up the struggle. We go to yoga to work on the things we need to work on, like being more gentle, being more patient, being more forgiving. We do the work on ourselves so we can give it to others. We may find ourselves in a challenging pose and start questioning ourselves. Yoga imitates life. Sometimes it's hard, sometimes it's rosy. Breathe!

"all-star yoga words" to infuse with your Intentions:

gentleness

acceptance

forgiveness

non-judgment

calmness

grace

faith

peace

and LOVE

Think of these words while in a difficult moment holding a yoga pose.

Yoga helps us find focus and clarity on the mat, which can then be carried off the mat. What we do on the mat is a direct reflection of how we live and approach life.

Intention One

Being Present: Are You Really Here?

SEAN

After injuries ended my football career, I did what most washed up athletes tend to do—spend countless hours dwelling on the past. For the next five years, I lived in the world known as "if only." If only I had trained a little differently, if only I had done this instead of that or... I spent my time thinking about the future and what I was going to do to replace my so-called football dream. I was paralyzed by my football dream.

The truth is that we spend a miniscule amount of our time living in the moment. The majority of the time we are caught in the past or looking toward the future. Preoccupied with what we've done, worrying about what's ahead, we disconnect ourselves from our own wisdom and end up in a "paralysis of analysis." Now, I look back and say "Wow, I did that! Really? How freaking lucky." How great it would have been if I had been totally present, feeling and living every moment. We all know about being somewhere but not really being there.

When we live in the present, we have nothing to prove. We don't have to perform or put on airs, because we have nothing to hide. Without dwelling on them, we accept our limitations—no more regretting our mistakes—and see in them opportunities for growth. We admit we're not perfect, and that's okay: everyone has flaws. Instead of trying to control other people, we decide to have faith in them and in ourselves and in this way, we accept responsibility for our own lives. No more "woe is me," nor making mountains out of molehills.

> Life is what happens while you're busy making other plans
>
> JOHN LENNON

> The Secret of health for both mind and body is not to mourn for the past, not to worry about the future, nor to anticipate troubles, but to live the present moment wisely and earnestly.
>
> BUDDHA

Remember when we were little tykes—five years old, let's say—and our teachers took attendance? Mitch Anderson? Here!... Abby Smith?... Here! Remember how enthusiastically we responded, how our hands shot into the air? If someone were to take roll now, how would we respond? Are we really here?

One afternoon, I was driving my kids home from school and asked my daughter about her day.

"Not so good, Dad. I got a demerit," she said.

"That's good," I replied.

"Dad, did you hear me?" she responded. "I got a demerit."

This is called being somewhere but not really being there.

To enjoy life's journey, we must be aware. Awareness is the key. Recently, my daughter and I went hiking together in Colorado, and I put her on camera duty. Walking along the trail, I admired the big pines and the grand peaks towering over us. She, on the other hand, noticed the small things. She would stop to take a picture of a single wildflower and think it the most beautiful flower she had ever seen. She noticed a small patch of luminous ice that had formed over a tiny creek. She discovered three twigs frozen and hovering above the ice, the tiniest lodgepole pine growing up through the snow.

THREE YOGIS IN A CAVE

Three Yogis are doing meditation in a remote cave. One day a sound is heard from outside the cave. After about six months, one of the yogis says, "Did you hear that goat?" Once again, there was silence. About a year later, one of the other Yogis says, "That wasn't a goat; it was a mule." Again, there was silence. About two years later the third yogi says, "If you two don't stop arguing, I'm leaving."

SEVEN WONDERS

Junior high school students in Chicago were asked to list what they considered to be the Seven Wonders of the World. Though there was some disagreement, the following received the most votes:

Egypt's Great Pyramids
The Taj Mahal in India
The Grand Canyon in Arizona
The Panama Canal
The Empire State Building
St. Peter's Basilica
China's Great Wall

While gathering the votes, the teacher noted that one student, a quiet girl, hadn't turned in her paper yet. So she asked the girl if she was having trouble with her list. The quiet girl replied, "Yes, a little. I couldn't quite make up my mind because there were so many." The teacher said, "Well, tell us what you have, and maybe we can help."

The girl hesitated, then read, "I think the Seven Wonders of the World are:

to touch...
to taste...
to see...
to hear... (She hesitated a little, and then added...)
to feel...
to laugh...
and to love.

The room was so quiet, you could have heard a pin drop.

The most wonderful things can be simple and ordinary. They may be right under our noses or inside of us. And we don't have to travel to faraway places to experience them. The wonders of life are surrounding us everyday. My father was a huge sports fan. He spent hours of his extra time watching sports, reading about sports, or listening to sports. To him they seemed very important. When he was diagnosed with

> The best time to plant a tree was 20 years ago. The second best time is now.
>
> **CHINESE PROVERB**

terminal colon cancer, his life changed overnight. He took on his first hobby that I ever saw: gardening. He decided to build a rock garden in his backyard and centered in the garden would be roses. Big, beautiful roses. He would collect various rocks during his travels, even in his last few months when his mind was waning. It was so uplifting and inspiring to watch him experience joy in gardens and roses. Just days before he died, my mother asked him if he could send her a sign after he died that he was OK, that he was in heaven. On the day he died, he was taken away by the gentlemen from the funeral home. At the moment my family stood on the front porch watching the hearse drive away, my mother became overwhelmed by the aroma of roses. She said the smell was so strong as if someone was pressing a rose right into your nostrils, and then we all smelled it.

Calm, decisive and focused, when we live in the present we handle stressful situations calmly. Because our minds are peaceful, we don't "freak out," and we are better able to communicate with others. We're okay with criticism, comfortable in our own skins. By freeing ourselves from the past, from regrets and anger over others' actions, we move forward without fear. By freeing ourselves from aspirations, from dreams of success or glory, we live without anxiety. Spontaneous and gentle, we learn more quickly.

The gift of happiness is in our hearts right now, just waiting to be opened. The more we give to our lives as they are, as we are, the more we receive. When we live in the present, we discover that nothing is missing, we are complete—we light up our own lives, we light up the world. When we pay full attention to the moment, we experience happiness because our experience is not muddied by past or future happenings.

A rich man complained to his friend: "People don't like me. They say I'm selfish and stingy. And yet in my last will and testament I have donated all that I own to charitable causes."

His friend said: "Well, maybe the story of the cow and the pig has a lesson for you."

The pig came to the cow and complained: 'People always talk about your friendliness. I know you are friendly, you do give them milk. But they get much, much more from me. They get ham and bacon and lard and they even cook my feet. And yet no one likes me. To all of them I am just a pig, a hog. Why is that?"

The cow thought it over a bit and then said: "Perhaps it's because I give while I am still alive!'"

> Normally, we do not so much look at things as overlook them.
>
> ALAN WATTS

The more you give to now, the more you get from now. The greatest gifts of life are always available to you here and now. Nothing is missing within you.

Mindfulness is living in the moment. When we are mindful, we operate with a heightened sense of awareness of our thoughts and actions. When our minds are somewhere else, hours pass right by us. It is next to impossible to be in the moment 100% of the time. However, by just practicing being more aware, we can live life with more joy. We think less of the past or future and live in the now."

Children are the best examples of being in the now. My 2-year-old loves trucks and trains. He'll play with them for hours. The whole time he gives all his attention to pushing the trucks around. He's not stressed thinking about what he has to do later or what happened to him yesterday. "Let the little children come to me," Jesus said, "for it is to those who are childlike that the Kingdom of Heaven belongs."

In this way, children can be our greatest teachers. They are free of habits and years of built up fears. We should attempt to emulate them. And by smiling, laughing, being spontaneous, and being creative, we are able to return to the ways of a child.

We have all experienced moments of being completely present. For example, I'm a big fan of coffee. I love it all: Guatemalan, Ethiopian, Costa Rican, Mexi-

> Watch your thoughts, they become words. Watch your words, they become actions. Watch your actions, they become habits. Watch your habits, they become character. Watch your character, it becomes your destiny!
>
> **UNKNOWN**

can, Kenyan. Sometimes when I drink my cup I can sit there and enjoy every part of it. I admire the espresso sitting in the froth. The sound of the spoon clinking on the saucer. The different flavors present in the coffee. On the other hand, sometimes I chug it and think about all the things I have to do that day. For some of us, it can be gardening where we are completely focused on nature and its boundless beauty. When you experience these moments, when you are completely "there," try to keep them flowing with everything you do. The next time you have a conversation with someone, look them right in the eyes and try to listen to every word they say without "reloading," without thinking about what you are going to say next.

When we are able to live being present, we experience happiness. When we consume our thoughts of yesterday and tomorrow, we can miss what is happening today. Instead of experiencing today, we just get through the day. Our minds can be everywhere and anywhere but not in that specific moment. Mindfulness is learning to be wherever you are. It is developing a unique focus on the current moment, and drawing from it all of the substance and wealth of experience and emotions that it has to offer. Being present is taking time to watch a sunset. Being present is listening to silence. Being present is capturing each moment so that it becomes a new part of what we are and of what we are in the process of becoming. Being present is not something we do; it is something we experience. Once we learn to be there, we master the art of living well.

Charles Plumb was a Navy jet pilot. On his 76th combat mission, he was shot down and parachuted into enemy territory. He was captured and spent six years in prison. He survived and now lectures on the lessons he learned from his experiences.

One day, a man in approached Plumb in a restaurant and said, "Are you Plumb, the navy pilot?"

"Yes, how did you know?" asked Plumb.

"I packed your parachute," the man replied.

Plumb was amazed—and grateful: "If the chute you packed hadn't worked I wouldn't be here today."

Plumb refers to this in his lectures—his realization that the anonymous sailors who packed the parachutes held the pilots' lives in their hands, and yet the pilots never gave these sailors a second thought; never even said hello, let alone said thanks.

Now Plumb asks his audiences, "Who packs your parachutes? Who helps you through your life—physically, mentally, emotionally, spiritually? Think about who helps you; recognise them and say thanks."

Sean's Amazing Yoga Tips for Practicing Presence on Your Mat

There is no better place to practice being present than on a yoga mat. When you are on your mat, honor the sensations that come up: feel what you feel. If you feel challenged, be okay with that; try to notice where you are tense and try to relax that part of your body. Try not to fidget. The poses may start out fidgety but over time we learn how to be still and quiet. Through the practice of yoga, we receive an opportunity to pay attention to how we react to what life throws at us. Try your best to relax into the sensation, to be patient with the process and with yourself. As best as you can, try to avoid "peoplewatchin-asana"—which is checking out other students during class. Keep your focus on your own mat. Listen to the sound of your breath, listen to your body, be gentle. Try sucking the juice out of every moment. When you are in the pose, really be in that pose. Try not be thinking of the next pose or spend time thinking about the last pose. Hear your breath, feel your breath moving through your body.

Intention Two

Slowing Down: Your Well-Being Will Thank You

KAREN

For many years, life was full of constant movement for me. As a kid, I was overactive and impatient. I struggled to sit still. How often during my school years had I heard that phrase "pay attention." Either I was distracted by what the person next to me was doing, or I drifted off into my own imagination. As I grew older, I still found myself addicted to being endlessly busy. I operated with a busy mind and a busy body, never taking time to smell the roses. Dance, running, and kickboxing gave me some relief, but when I took my first yoga class it was different. Yoga was more than a physical outlet—it gave me the tools to see clearly, to actually slow down and listen.

We all yearn for experiences that help buffer the hustle and bustle of a hurried world. The world we live in is incredibly stressful. We greet friends by telling them how busy we are, as if we are nothing more than our schedules, a list of things to do. Sometimes it seems as if we are competing with one another to see who is busier. Caught up in the rat race, we get distracted by the demands of our everyday lives—grocery shopping, paying bills, driving the kids here and there. I see new students arrive at the yoga studio scattered and staring around. They beat themselves up trying to keep pace with the class because they are in such a hurry to get to the next pose.

This is why we need yoga. We need to pause and observe the insanity we create for ourselves. When we learn to practice the slowing down between impulse and reaction we discover that we can choose how to respond. As we take care of ourselves, we find that we are actually better able to function at work, better able to care for others. As we slow down, we gain access to something higher, and we begin to see more clearly why we are on the planet. Yoga is about being good to ourselves so that we can be of service to the world. In this way, we learn that everything depends on our health. If we want true health, we need to find ways of feeling good. Yoga becomes a treasure map to the self, to the treasure inside.

This entire obsession over being busy in our lives has led to unprecedented health problems for many people. If we do not listen to our bodies or to our intuition (which is begging us to slow down!), we may find ourselves with poor health conditions brought on by stress. By living the "fast life," we accelerate the aging process. We can also experience anxiety, depression, and other emotional illnesses.

All the advances in technology—texting, internet—have freed up time for us. But what we have done is decided to fill those minutes up to become even more busy. We go about our days being over-scheduled and stressed, always moving towards the next thing to do. Not only are we busy at work, we eat at a hectic pace and even our vacations have become over-scheduled. Luckily, many of us are noticing this and this is the first step: being aware of our hurriedness. By reconnecting to nature and the rhythmic flow of life, we can recapture moments. When we operate slowly, we are living a more connected life. Once we slow down, our lives become balanced. It is a more mindful way to live. We start to savor food, linger with friends and family. We move from human doings back to human beings.

One day, an expert in time management was speaking to a group of business students and, to drive home a point, used an illustration those students will never forget. As he stood in front of the group of high-powered overachievers he said, "Okay, time for a quiz"

> A busy mind is a sick mind.
> A slow mind is a healthy mind.
> A still mind is a divine mind.
>
> **NATIVE AMERICAN PROVERB**

and he pulled out a one-gallon, wide-mouth mason jar and set it on the table in front of him. He also produced about a dozen fist-sized rocks and carefully placed them, one at a time, into the jar. When the jar was filled to the top and no more rocks would fit inside, he asked, "Is this jar full?" Everyone in the class yelled, "Yes." The time management expert replied, "Really?" He reached under the table and pulled out a bucket of gravel. He dumped some gravel in and shook the jar causing pieces of gravel to work themselves down into the spaces between the big rocks. He then asked the group once more, "Is the jar full?" By this time the class was on to him. "Probably not," one of them answered. "Good!" he replied. He reached under the table and brought out a bucket of sand. He started dumping the sand in the jar and it went into all of the spaces left between the rocks and the gravel. Once more he asked the question, "Is this jar full?" "No!" the class shouted. Once again he said, "Good." Then he grabbed a pitcher of water and began to pour it in until the jar was filled to the brim. Then he looked at the class and asked, "What is the point of this illustration?" One eager beaver raised his hand and said, "The point is, no matter how full your schedule is, if you try really hard you can always fit some more things in it!" "No," the speaker replied, "that's not the point. The truth this illustration teaches us is, 'If you don't put the big rocks in first, you'll never get them in at all.' What are the big rocks in your life? Time with loved ones, your faith, your education, your dreams, a worthy cause, teaching or mentoring others? Remember to put these big rocks in first or you'll never get them in at all. So, tonight, or in the morning, when you are reflecting on this short story, ask yourself this question, 'What are the big rocks in my life?' Then, put those in your jar first."

I recently had a student ask me if I noticed how frequently he was taking rests in his practice. He then told me it was his birthday so he was taking it easy this evening. In life, we don't need to wait for our birthday or a special occasion to give ourselves the extra break we need. We somehow feel that we need an excuse to relax and take it easy. One of the most valuable things we can do for our health is to practice moderation. As Americans we been taught to think that being busy means we are successful, but the truth is that your job and your schedule don't take care of you if you become ill. Our fast-paced lives have robbed us of the important things: connecting to our friends and loved ones. We need to start listening to that small voice inside trying to urge us to slow down.

The physical practice never gets easy, but we learn to move with greater ease.

One day, I was at the studio getting ready for a yoga practice when I received a high alert text from my daughter. She hadn't been too excited about attending a camp where she didn't know anybody, and her roommate hadn't shown up the first night or the next day. Now it looked like she was going to be spending a second night alone.

After her first night without a roommate, she and I both thought she would not have to spend another night solo in the dorm. So when this text arrived, I started to panic. One night of solitude built character, but a whole week seemed like a mean joke. I was ready to dart out of yoga and drive to the camp. Instead, I got on my mat. Scattered and upset, regretting that I'd said everything would be okay, it took a while to settle down.

If you are a parent, you know that strong impulse to protect your children. It's inscribed in your DNA. But I've also learned that I make better decisions after yoga. I remembered that it's not what happens to us, but how we react that matters, and I recognized that I was charged up about something relatively small. As I began to breathe and move, I started to settle down and have that third person conversation with myself. It would all work out. I'd call and talk with someone at the camp and it would be okay.

This doesn't mean that yoga solves everything, but it opens us to the idea that life is not a sprint. Life is a marathon and the more we relax and pace ourselves,

> We're going slower in order to go deeper, in order to go faster in the direction of urgently needed change.
>
> **MARIANNE WILLIAMSON**

the easier it is to find our way and the less likely we are to get burned out early in the race. Breathing is like a telescope or microscope that makes the invisible visible, that allows us to see what has been there all along. We just need to turn the instrument on to discover that space between each breath where love and light reside. Of course, by the time I got back to my phone that day, my daughter had solved the problem on her own.

On my way to the studio one evening after getting out of work late, worried I wouldn't make it to class on time, I rushed around the corner of one of the narrow side streets in Shadyside and got into a fender bender. The other driver had never been in an accident before, and neither had I, so, we fumbled through our glove compartments and exchanged insurance information. She was very understanding and calm about the whole situation. I, on the other hand, was a mess.

After she left, I sat in my car for a moment and had a mini-breakdown. I called my husband and he asked if there was any damage to the car or if I was hurt. I said no, and he asked why I was worrying so much. I guess it seemed like the right thing to do after a car accident. After I hung up, I looked at my watch and realized I still had plenty of time to get to my yoga class. I almost turned around and drove home, but I knew I would just sit around feeling bad for the rest of the night, so I buckled my seatbelt and continued on to yoga, where I ended up having one of the most relaxing practices ever.

The funny part about the whole situation is that I was so stressed and anxious to get to yoga that I ended up causing a car accident on the way there, but I still had plenty of time to get to class. This taught me that the calmness and mindfulness that we practice on the mat is something we need to practice in our daily lives as well. Had I remained calm even though I was running late and knocked off my routine a bit, the accident probably would never have happened.

—Julie

Younger children have a natural way of being in the rhythm of life. They don't feel the pressures of deadlines or the hurriedness of a schedule to keep. You watch how they don't need to rush from one toy to the next. They move on when they are ready. Kids simply engage themselves fully with their toys and their friends. They are in no hurry to leave the playground or go onto the next thing. They are in rhythm with life. As we grow, somehow we lose that ability to be in the moment, to travel at a pace that seems healthy. We take on more than we can handle, we overfill our calendars and rush from one thing to the next, missing out on all the fun to be had along the way. Life is to be enjoyed, not endured.

> There is nothing that wastes the body like worry, and one who has any faith in God should be ashamed to worry about anything whatsoever.
>
> GANDHI

A young and successful executive was traveling down a neighborhood street, going a bit too fast in his new Jaguar. He was watching for kids darting out from between parked cars and slowed down when he thought he saw something. As his car passed, no children appeared. Instead, a brick smashed into the Jag's side door. He slammed on the brakes and backed the Jag back to the spot where the brick had been thrown. The angry driver then jumped out of the car, grabbed the nearest kid and pushed him up against a parked car shouting, "What was that all about and who are you? Just what the heck are you doing? That's a new car and that brick you threw is going to cost a lot of money. Why did you do it?" The young boy was apologetic. "Please, mister...please! I'm sorry but I didn't know what else to do," he pleaded. "I threw the brick because no one else would stop." With tears dripping down his face and off his chin, the youth pointed to a spot just around a parked car. "It's my brother," he said. "He rolled off the curb and fell out of his wheelchair and I can't lift him up." Now sobbing, the boy asked the stunned executive, "Would you please help me get him back into his wheelchair? He's hurt and he's too heavy for me." Moved beyond words, the driver tried to swallow the rapidly swelling lump in his throat. He hurriedly lifted the handicapped boy back into the wheelchair, then took out a linen handkerchief and dabbed at the fresh scrapes and cuts. A quick look told him everything was going to be okay. "Thank you and may God bless you," the grateful child told the stranger. Too shook up for words, the man simply watched the boy push his wheelchair-bound brother down the sidewalk toward their home. It was a long, slow walk back to the Jaguar. The damage was very noticeable, but the driver never bothered to repair the dented side door. He kept the dent there to remind him of this message: "Don't go through life so fast that someone has to throw a brick at you to get your attention."

Recently, our family went to a concert. Music, like yoga, has a way of revealing your connection to life's natural rhythm. Watching my children, I saw how this naturalness gets tougher with age. When you are two years old, you feel free in the music. At six, you dance for others to watch. At 11, you still want to play, but you are a little afraid of what others may think. By the time you are 14, you're just worried about being cool.

Slowing down is a conscious choice and not always an easy one, but it leads to a greater appreciation for life and a greater level of happiness. Yoga helps us return to our purest selves. We reclaim our natural rhythm. When we practice yoga, we take away the masks we've worn to look good. Instead, life becomes natural and honest. Don't miss it! Choosing to feel small and insignificant is not an option. We need to move out of the dullness of our schedules and live life brightly. Reclaim your life, and discover the difference between just living and living authentically. Live the life you are meant to live! Slow down and reconnect. No one on their deathbed wishes they had spent more time at the office.

A YOGA STUDENT'S STORY

As a mother of three boys, twin one-year-olds and a toddler, my typical day is consumed with requests, needs and tasks.

When I come to the mat during child's pose, and ready myself for the next 90 minutes, I feel the thoughts of my day begin to drift away. As class progresses, I listen to the comforting voice of the teacher, the collective sound of the class breathing, and I notice my limbs extending farther than I thought possible. In these quiet moments, and during rest after exertion, I feel rejuvenated and awake.

Many of my friends who don't know about yoga notice that I have lost my pregnancy pounds. But I tell them that this is the least of what I have lost. I have lost the clutter of distracting thoughts and the burden of constant urgency. And I have gained so much more. Patience for my children, more energy to create and learn with them, and more affection and tenderness for my husband. The ultimate testimony is that my stressed, businessman husband has picked up yoga as well, and loves it.

People ask me, why do you seem so calm given all the demands of having three children under the age of three? They ask, what is your secret? I tell them it's as easy as breathing. I do something anyone can do....I practice yoga (and more yoga).

—Diane

We have all seen the car weaving in and out of traffic with the driver's face serious and tense. They continue to cut people off and move their car in quick jerks just to get ahead of a few people. Then 20 minutes later, as you get through the traffic jam, you look over to your left and see that person sitting right next to you at the light, and their face is still tense and angry because they never got any further along than the rest of us. We think that if we rush the process, we will come out a step ahead, but mostly we just arrive more frustrated and anxious.

Karen's Amazing Yoga Tips for Slowing Down on Your Mat

Take a deep breath and don't worry about having to get all the poses just perfect. Don't let the physical practice of yoga become one more thing to accomplish or achieve. The real beauty of this practice is slowing down enough that you can feel how powerful being at ease in a challenging pose can be. The practice of yoga starts with the breath, then we add some movements to the breathing: if you feel a calm relaxed breath in every pose, you are soaking up all the juice of this moment. Pay attention to the depth of your breathing in every posture; if it is deep and free, you are traveling through the practice at the right pace. Like anything, the more you drive your body, the faster it wears out

Intention Three

Contentment: Let's Be Happy

SEAN

We are the wealthiest nation in the world, yet so many of us are unhappy. It's almost as if we have everything, yet we feel as if we have nothing. We pour time and energy into looking good and worrying about what other people think of us. We say to ourselves, "When I get what I want, then I'll be happy." All this wanting is just accumulating "stuff," some of it physical, some of it "accomplishments." The funny thing is, while we worry about what other people think, they fret over our judgments of them—we're all obsessing about each other, focused outward rather than on ourselves. Then we get those things—a better job, a new car, a toned body—and we still feel empty. We want more and more. "I want to scuba dive, I want to climb Mt. Everest, I want a bigger car, I want others to find me interesting." It's a habitual pattern, an addiction.

The ego defines itself by what it possesses, and it always wants more. Attaching itself to job success, body image and social status, the ego is a seeker that never finds. Living in the past or the future but never in the now, the ego thrives on fear, resentment, anxiety, and reactivity. The ego's doubts are very loud—they deny your inner happiness, suffocate your inner wisdom. We need to differentiate between our ego (fears and doubts) and our inner wisdom (the voice of reason, love and joy). To do so is to take a big step toward connecting, instead of competing with others. Wealth, beauty and success can't bring us peace. Focus on collecting moments instead of things.

Let's move out of our day-to-day habits. Sure, not wanting the other stuff is hard. Desire builds until we confront it, until we challenge ourselves to do something else. But to be free, we've got to release ourselves from the ego's needs. Yoga doesn't care how you look in a bikini. Yoga doesn't care if you can touch your toes. Yoga just asks you to tap into your inner voice and listen. We can quash the ego by practicing awareness, by smiling and laughing. Because when you move through life comfortable in your own skin, you radiate joy and possess magnetism. People will want to be around you. We end up living a balanced life, happy and healthy—isn't that what we all want to be?

There was once a stonecutter who was dissatisfied with himself and with his position in life. One day he passed a wealthy merchant's house. Through the open gateway, he saw many fine possessions and important visitors. "How powerful that merchant must be!" thought the stonecutter.

He became very envious and wished that he could be like the merchant. To his great surprise, he suddenly became the merchant, enjoying more luxuries and power than he had ever imagined, but he was envied and detested by those less wealthy than himself. Soon a high official passed by, carried in a sedan chair, accompanied by attendants and escorted by soldiers beating gongs. Everyone, no matter how wealthy, had to bow low before the procession.

"How powerful that official is!" he thought. "I wish that I could be a high official!" Then he became the high official, carried everywhere in his embroidered sedan chair, feared and hated by the people all around. It was a hot summer day, so the official felt very uncomfortable in the sticky sedan chair. He looked up at the sun. It shone proudly in the sky, unaffected by his presence.

"How powerful the sun is!" he thought. "I wish that I could be the sun!" Then he became the sun, shining fiercely down on everyone, scorching the fields,

cursed by the farmers and laborers. But a huge black cloud moved between him and the earth, so that his light could no longer shine on everything below.

"How powerful that storm cloud is!" he thought. "I wish that I could be a cloud!" Then he became the cloud, flooding the fields and villages, shouted at by everyone. But soon he found that he was being pushed away by some great force, and realized that it was the wind.

"How powerful it is!" he thought. "I wish that I could be the wind!" Then he became the wind, blowing tiles off the roofs of houses, uprooting trees, feared and hated by all below him. But after a while, he ran up against something that would not move, no matter how forcefully he blew against it – a huge, towering rock.

"How powerful that rock is!" he thought. "I wish that I could be a rock!" Then he became the rock, more powerful than anything else on earth. But as he stood there, he heard the sound of a hammer pounding a chisel into the hard surface, and felt himself being changed.

"What could be more powerful than I, the rock?" he thought. He looked down and saw far below him the figure of a stonecutter.

Many of us spend our entire lives chasing after elusive dreams of happiness. We end up missing the moments and the full lives we already have. Instead of finding joy in the simple things, we take them for granted. And we find ourselves always looking for greener pastures. We talk ourselves into believing that our lives will be happy once we are married. Then, we will be happy once we have a baby. Then, we are not happy because we have realized that we are getting older. Then, we'll be happy when we have an exotic car. But, in reality, there is no better time to be happy than right at this very moment.

When we live from a place of contentment, we are practicing being happy in the present moment. Most of us think of the word contentment as meaning just

> Enjoy the little things, for one day you may look back and realize they were the big things.
>
> ROBERT BRAULT

> For a long time it had seemed to me that life was about to begin—real life. But there was always some obstacle in the way, something to be gotten through first, some unfinished business, time still to be served, a debt to be paid. Then life would begin. At last it dawned on me that these obstacles were my life.
>
> ALFRED D'SOUZA

being satisfied with what you have. We don't dwell on the past and we don't fantasize about the future. Being content means you are happy and comfortable in your own skin. As we all know, it is almost impossible to keep our minds out of the past and peeking towards the future. But when we focus our thoughts on what could happen, we spend countless hours of our precious time.

The opposite of contentment is wanting. This wanting or desire is what drags our attention to either the past or future. Wanting can be endless; if we stay stuck in wanting, we stay stuck in unhappiness. When we are able to restrain our desires to have more, we can discover happiness. When we move blindly obsessing about our desires, we can miss out on precious moments with loved ones. Wanting fills our minds with obsessive thoughts that pull our focus away from the present. We spend an enormous amount of time having internal conversations concerned with wanting. By being ok with where we are, we can experience spontaneity, joy, creativity, and bliss. We can invite in our spiritual wisdom.

Some of us become upset when we start to compare ourselves to others. We have our health, we have friends, we live in a beautiful world. But we are still unhappy. We tell ourselves, "I cannot be happy today." We count our friends or possessions and see that some have more than we do. It troubles us. We may be happy with our current number of friends or possessions, but we tell ourselves that we would be happier if we had more. But happiness is happiness. It cannot be measured. It cannot be counted. We must learn to recognize it when we have it. We must be content with it. If we have bad days that are filled with struggle and absent of joy, we must remain content and patient because happiness is there and it will come again if we let it.

Contentment gives you the ability to be comfortable wherever you are, in all circumstances. Past and future are stilled, and you can have full enjoyment in the moment.

Once we move away from constant wanting, we realize that we possess great self-control. Most of us think that people who practice self-control are missing out on life's great things. But actually they are living a life of freedom. Freedom from attachment. It is quite liberating and powerful.

Being content is extremely hard when we are sad or grieving. We struggle to think of anything else except our loss. We all go through this at one time or another. When we lose someone, we think of all of our great memories with them. We also think of the experiences that we will miss with them in the future. To get through it, we should enter the present moment which gives us contentment, which leads to gratitude for that loved one and what s/he shared with us. It gives us the strength and courage to keep moving, to keep loving, to keep sharing.

One who focuses on contentment lives a peaceful life.

Contentment is not spiritual complacency but acceptance of the situation that we are allotted in this life. With contentment, we are accepting the current state as it truly is. We are using what we have instead of operating with the ego, which forcefully pushes its way around.

GOD'S COFFEE

A group of alumni, highly established in their careers, got to talking at a reunion and decided to go visit their old university professor, now retired.

During their visit, conversation soon turned into complaints about stress in their work and lives. Offering his guests coffee, the professor went to the kitchen and returned with a large pot of coffee and an assortment of cups—porcelain, plastic, glass, crystal, some plain-looking, some expensive, some exquisite—telling them to help themselves to the coffee.

When all the alumni had a cup of coffee in hand, the professor said, 'Notice that all the nice-looking, expen-

> sive cups were taken up, leaving behind the plain and cheap ones. While it is normal for you to want only the best for yourselves, that is the source of your problems and stress. Be assured that the cup itself adds no quality to the coffee. In most cases, it is just more expensive and in some cases even hides what we drink.
>
> What all of you really wanted was coffee, not the cup, but you consciously went for the best cups... and then you began eying each other's cups.
>
> Now consider this: Life is the coffee; your job, money and position in society are the cups. They are just tools to hold and contain Life. The type of cup one has does not define nor change the quality of Life a person lives. Sometimes, by concentrating only on the cup, we fail to enjoy the coffee God has provided us.
>
> The happiest of people don't necessarily have the best of everything; they just make the most of everything that comes along their way.
>
> God brews the coffee, not the cups... Enjoy your coffee.

We tend to forget that happiness doesn't come as a result of getting something we don't have, but rather of recognizing and appreciating what we do have.

FREDERICK KEONIG

So many people are unhappy these days that we actually think something is wrong with those who always appear happy. If they are constantly smiling we suspect that they are crazy; if they are praying to God, then they are "too religious." But true happiness is an inner power that we all possess, a power available to us that heals and allows us to live in abundance. We're looking for spiritual advancement. If we want to be happy, let's try making other people happy.

Buddha discovered that you don't have to travel far to find peace and love. The "Inside-Out Approach" means not looking to the outside world for liberation or happiness, but instead taking responsibility for oneself and becoming what we seek: happiness, health, peace. Looking within oneself to find inspiration and power, and then acting from this place. Buddha knew that no one can save us but ourselves. We must walk our own path.

Karen and I once went to Africa. During a safari in Kenya, we decided to visit one of the local villages. As we approached the village, we noticed that it gave off an unpleasant odor. The homes were simply small huts made out of branches, mud and cow dung. We entered one of the huts, which was no bigger than the size of a three-man tent. In the hut were two mothers and six kids. And something else: eight smiling faces.

A STUDENT'S STORY

I practice Amazing Yoga because it requires all of my strength, concentration, balance, and acceptance. My body continues to be sculpted by each session on the mat. I am stronger than I have ever been. Yoga requires me to be "fully present" so that I am becoming more aware of each minute both on and off the mat. Each time I come into a balancing pose, I must learn where my body is at that moment and where it will choose to settle. The balance allows me to pick myself up and realize that right where I am today is enough. I am learning to accept that every time I practice yoga, I am not trying to be the best at yoga. It's a funny thing to write because it seems so simple, but it asks so much of a person's ego to show up on a mat every day and continue to practice poses and meditations and breathing that will never become "perfect". I consider myself an athlete but I will never score the most poses or win the most flexibility points and the best part of yoga is realizing that is just fine.

—*LeeAnne*

> It has been my observation that people are just about as happy as they make up their minds to be.
>
> ABRAHAM LINCOLN

I set some lofty goals growing up. One was that I would be successful and therefore happy if I became a professional football player. I began playing football at eight years old and had great success immediately. I was obsessed with this dream; I kicked hundreds of balls every week. Even the harsh winters in Erie wouldn't stop my one-track mind. I would trudge ten blocks in three feet of snow with my bag of balls and cleats and kick on the ice that covered the field during the winter months. When I was growing up, we got so much snow that the entire lake froze and people walked across the lake to Canada.

After completing high school, I was not offered a scholarship so I decided to attend a small school in Pennsylvania with the hopes of transferring later. I had an appointment to meet the coach in which they would get me outfitted with pads, a locker, etc. The coach didn't show. So I made another appointment to meet him the next day. Again, he didn't show. So I got the hint; I wasn't wanted. Because I thought my football dream was tanking, I turned to alcohol (received a DUI and spent time at a weekend rehab center) and my grades of course plummeted. I ended the semester with a less than impressive 1.33 GPA. So I quit school and moved home and sank into a deep depression. I was 19 and all of my friends were in college having a ball, doing what college kids do, and I was working a minimum wage job. I spent countless hours wishing and hoping for what I could have. But after months of being depressed, I realized my outlook on life, not the situation, was causing my unhappiness.

It is up to us to choose to be happy. Certainly there are exceptions but for the most part it holds true. We all have had moments were we felt our lives were crappy. We have moments where our job is less than ideal, we experience challenges in relationships or we have financial burdens, or we are discouraged with our weight.

To lift from those places of unhappiness, we can elevate ourselves by our attitude and our thoughts. Typically, when we are unhappy we are focusing on all the happenings in our lives that are not going well. We usually fall into the "woe is me" attitude. Why can't I have a boyfriend when all my friends do? Or why can't I afford a BMW when everyone else on the block has one? We can end up in a place of paralysis where we cease to move forward with our lives. This paralysis can lead to depression. Our negative energy can start to spread to the people around us. Overall, it just makes matters worse.

Contentment is coming to the realization of how much we already possess. When we are happy, we are typically focusing on the positive in our lives. We may be experiencing challenges in our lives but we look at the bright side and we are happy for the things that we do have. A job that pays the bills, health, family, and friends. It's the simple act of counting our blessings. This kind of outlook can completely change our perspective on life. When we live with a positive outlook, everything around us thrives: our families, our relationships, our jobs, our health.

> Man's happiness really lies in contentment.
>
> GANDHI

THE HUNT FOR HAPPINESS

A thirsty poet was walking in the woods one night when he came upon a well with a bucket and an attached rope. He looked into the well and the vision that met his eyes made his heart stop momentarily. Although a man accustomed to waxing lyrical about almost anything, he found no words to describe the beauty of the tranquil, perfectly round object, shimmering with ivory light at the bottom of the well.

Determined that such a dazzling thing should be his, he lowered the bucket into the well and tried to "catch" the object. The instant the bucket touched the water, the thing of beauty began to waver and distort. The poet brought up several buckets full of water, but the object remained at the bottom of the well. After the ripples had settled, it seemed to mock him with its serenity and inertia.

Undeterred, the poet labored the entire night until finally he had emptied the well. He looked down and was shocked to see that the vision of beauty was no longer there. Worn out and distraught, he fell on his back, bemoaning his loss. At that moment, he saw the fading moon in the sky making way for the morning sun and finally understood his folly.

By practicing a simple life instead of a consuming life we can lead a life of contentment. Consuming can consist of accomplishments, awards and levels of success. When we live a simple life, we make decisions consciously knowing that we don't need more of something.

Sean's Amazing Yoga Tips for Practicing Contentment on Your Mat

Make every effort to avoid turning your yoga practice into a competition with others or most importantly, yourself. Try not to compare your body with those in the room. Try not to worry about how the poses look. When we move away from "not wanting," we find ourselves in a place of contentment. In yoga, we can practice this contentment by holding a pose and focusing on the experience of it instead of the desire of trying to perfect it. Don't worry about mastering so-called "advanced poses." There is no spiritual advancement for those who can stand on their hands. In yoga, there are no bonus plans, no performance reviews, no expectations. If you ever wonder how your yoga practice is working for you, if you can manage a smile during each yoga class, it's heading in the right direction! Remember, there's no place to get, just a place to be. Keep your focus on being happy and healthy. Remind yourself what an amazing thing you are doing for yourself. There is no right way or wrong way. It's your way. It's got to feel good. Make sure you are having fun, that you are feeling good.

> Do what you can, with what you have, where you are.
>
> **THEODORE ROOSEVELT**

Intention Four

Non-Violence: Be a Peaceful Warrior

KAREN

When we are new to yoga, we feel how wonderful a sweaty physical practice can be. We think, "If I feel this good after 75 minutes, maybe if I do more I will feel even better." Our culture tells us that if a little of something is good, more will certainly be better. We gobble up as much as we can. But yoga is about practicing moderation, strengthening our bodies and minds while resisting the urge to go all out, burn out, and move on.

Yoga's aim is emotional and physical balance. When we are practicing yoga, and not just working out, we listen not to our intellect or ego, but to our intuition. We notice how we actually feel.

Ashley was a Division I gymnast and runner in college. Afterward, she became a personal trainer. "For so many years, I considered myself well-informed about wellness and fitness, yet for many years I did strenuous exercise that likely did more harm to my body than good. I also did nothing to stay connected on a spiritual level. Now, I practice yoga at least twice a week, wherever my job takes me, and it has changed my life. I am in better physical shape than ever and yoga has helped restore my alignment and nagging lower back pain. I also suffer from Interstitial Cystitis, a chronic condition exacerbated by stress, and yoga has helped me keep this condition suppressed."

Some days, we need to modify our practices to meet our bodies' needs. By honoring the sensations that arise, by listening rather than following some idea of what we should do, we create a peaceful relation-

> Non-violence is not a garment to be put on and off at will.
> Its seat is in the heart, and it must be an inseparable part of our being.
>
> **GANDHI**

ship with ourselves. This is where the practice of non-violence, "ahimsa," begins. We realize that what we say to ourselves can be uplifting or damaging. If the voice inside you is always repeating, "you are not good enough as you are," or "things never work out for me," then you are filling every cell of your being with negativity. Not only does this not feel good, but we are a manifestation of our thoughts. We must first practice love, kindness and patience with ourselves and then we will be able to extend these qualities to the world.

When we practice yoga, we participate in a tradition of connecting with others, a lineage rooted in freedom and liberation. Thus, when we speak of non-harming or "ahimsa," we are talking about something much deeper than not hurting others physically. We are speaking of compassion and kindness, to others and ourselves. Violence, after all, takes many forms. Consider how easily we pollute the earth on which we live or say something rude without thinking. Consider how often we think unkindly of ourselves. Violence--judgment, criticism, anger, irritation—stems from fear and when we are afraid, we are unable to forgive. We build walls around our hearts. Negative emotions cloud our view, like a dirty lens through which we can no longer see the good. This is why, as Proust wrote, "The real act of discovery is not in finding new lands, but in seeing with new eyes."

We don't have to give up meat or become social activists to practice non-violence: there are so many small, everyday actions we can take. Patanjali says in the Yoga Sutras that non-violence is "abstention from harming others," not just acts of harm, but thoughts of judgment and jealousy. There's a wonderful story attributed to the Buddha:

Buddha was traveling in the company of several other people. One of the travelers began to test Buddha by responding to anything he said with disparaging, insulting, hurtful remarks. Every day for the next three days, this traveler verbally abused Buddha, call-

ing him a fool, arrogantly ridiculing him in any way he could.

Finally, after three days, the rude traveler could stand it no longer. He asked Buddha, "How can you continue to be so kind and loving when all I've done for the last three days is dishonor, offend and try to find ways to hurt you? Each time I try to hurt you, you respond in a kind manner? How can this be?"

Buddha responded with a question for his fellow traveler, "If someone offers you a gift, and you do not accept that gift, to whom does the gift belong?"

> When you judge another, you do not define them, you define yourself.
>
> WAYNE DYER

It takes a great deal of discipline to refrain from reacting negatively to others, let alone refrain from thinking negatively. Yet simply becoming aware of how we affect others is an important start. Through the physical practice of yoga, we purify our relationship with ourselves and learn that how we treat others mirrors how we treat ourselves. The real practice of yoga is about getting good with ourselves so we can get good with others, about seeing others as we want to be seen. In this way, the world is refreshed.

In the mid-1980s, Dr. John Davies and his colleagues wanted to study the effects of meditation not just on the practitioners themselves, but on people nearby, on what the Maharishi Mahesh Yogi described as the "collective consciousness." Thus, Davies invited a group of mediators large enough, according to the Maharishi's theory, to affect the people of southern Lebanon, then embroiled in civil war. According to Davies:

> During these periods of meditation, average fatalities in Lebanon dropped by more than 70% (the probability that these results were due to chance was less than one in a hundred billion), and in Israel the level of violence (crime, car accidents and fires) dropped significantly. . . People came together in a spirit of cooperation and partnership (an increase of 66%), and progress was made in mediation and agreement between Lebanon, Syria and Israel. Unfortunately, when the meditating group disbanded or the numbers dropped significantly below the threshold size, this progress fell apart.

Just as we never know the full impact of our damaging words and actions, we never know how far our positive influence may travel. We have to trust that whatever we do—good and bad alike—touches others. By practicing non-violence, we acknowledge that we are all in this together, that our actions matter, that we have an impact on the world.

A soldier was finally coming home after having fought in Vietnam. He called his parents from San Francisco. "Mom and Dad, I'm coming home, but I've a favor to ask. I have a friend I'd like to bring home with me."

"Sure," they replied, "we'd love to meet him."

"There's something you should know," the son continued, "he was hurt pretty badly in the fighting. He stepped on a land mine and lost an arm and a leg. He has nowhere else to go, and I want him to come live with us."

"I'm sorry to hear that, son. Maybe we can help him find somewhere to live."

"No, Mom and Dad, I want him to live with us."

"Son," said the father, "you don't know what you're asking. Someone with such a handicap would be a terrible burden on us. We have our own lives to live, and we can't let something like this interfere with our lives. I think you should just come home and forget about this guy. He'll find a way to live on his own."

At that point, the son hung up the phone. The parents heard nothing more from him. A few days later, however, they received a call from the San Francisco police. Their son had died after falling from a building, they were told. The police believed it was suicide. The grief-stricken parents flew to San Francisco and were taken to the city morgue to identify the body of their son. They recognized him, but to their horror they also discovered something they didn't know, their son had only one arm and one leg.

The parents in this story are like many of us. We find it easy to love those who are good-looking or fun to have around, but we don't like people who inconvenience us or make us feel uncomfortable. We would rather stay away from people who aren't as healthy, beautiful or smart as we are.

There is a type of poison known as mind poison. We are all aware of the horrible effects of talking about others in ways that are not complimentary. We have all done it, and we have all been victims of gossip.

A few years ago, I really started to take notice of how easy it is to categorize and share my take on this or that person. I noticed how initially it is exciting and fun feeling a sense of social bonding, and then later I would have a terrible sense of regret and shame at what I had said. The awareness of how this has affected me has been the first step towards being careful about what I say and how I say it.

There is power in our thoughts and words. If you have very strong angry thoughts directed at a person, you send off an enormous amount of negative energy. The opposite is also true: when you send loving kindness towards someone, you can have a positive effect on that person. The principle of non-violence is that we must stay aware of our words and our thoughts so that they do not harm others.

I was crying into my sweaty towel during what had to be my third or fourth half-pigeon ever while my yoga instructor talked about muscles housing emotional pain. I listened to her simple description of this pain as I wiped my eyes, hoping people thought it was sweat, not tears.

It was all my mother's fault. She was the first one to take me to yoga. Normally she had to drag me to things—school, dinner, shopping, and usually it ended in both of us red-faced, hands in the air, knocked-down and dragged-out angry. But I don't remember any hesitation at her mention of yoga. I considered myself a bit of a hippie so yoga seemed like a cool thing to do. But the class was no hippie-peace-love-meditation-and-hug-your-neighbor yoga. It was hot, for starters, and it was hard.

At the age of 16, I hated my body. It betrayed me more than once, and so I hurt myself, determined to become either stronger or uglier. I wore long sleeves to hide my shame.

That first class, as sweat dripped down my back and into my eyes, something inside me stirred. There was a creature, a light, inside of me that started to grow as the heat in my belly grew. Each inhale ignited it; each exhale filled my limbs with its life. So I kept going. My mother and I found we had something to talk about. We made it through the wretchedly cold Pittsburgh winter with the heat of the yoga room as our weekly retreat. And the body I hated changed, too. I realized I had confused strength with the hardness that pain makes. It took real strength to treat myself with gentleness and love.

It's been nine years since that first yoga class. Occasionally I look at my scars and wonder where I would be without yoga. Occasionally I sink down into half-pigeon and hear that instructor's voice telling me to let go, and a knot wells up in my throat. It happens less and less these days. I like to think it's because I'm living a happier, cleaner life now that my body has been cleansed of its old hardships. Perhaps I was destined to find yoga, or perhaps my mother really does know what's best for me.

--Candace

THE TEST OF THREE (TRUTH, GOODNESS AND USEFULNESS)

One day, Socrates came upon an acquaintance that ran up to him excitedly and said, "Socrates, do you know what I just heard about one of your students?"

"Wait a moment," Socrates replied. "Before you tell me I'd like you to pass a little test. It's called the Test of Three."

"Three?"

"That's right," Socrates continued "Before you talk to me about my student let's take a moment to test what you're going to say. The first test is Truth. Have you made absolutely sure that what you are about to tell me is true?"

"No," the man said, "actually I just heard about it."

"All right," said Socrates. "So you don't really know if it's true or not. Now let's try the second test, the test of Goodness. Is what you are about to tell me about my student something good?"

"No, on the contrary..."

"So," Socrates continued, "you want to tell me something bad about him even though you're not certain it's true?"

The man shrugged, a little embarrassed.

Socrates continued. "You may still pass though, because there is a third test—the filter of Usefulness. Is what you want to tell me about my student going to be useful to me?"

"No, not really."

"Well," concluded Socrates, "if what you want to tell me is neither True nor Good nor even Useful, why tell it to me at all?"

> He who throws mud only loses ground.
>
> FAT ALBERT

Karen's Amazing Yoga Tips for Practicing Non-Violence on Your Mat

We can easily apply the concept of ahimsa on our yoga mats by practicing mindfulness and compassion towards ourselves. Trying not to push our bodies into places that they are not ready to go because we think we should. Feeling fatigued but pushing on because we don't want to be seen as quitters. Treat your body like the prized possession it is: when we move out of the intellect and approach our practice from a place of mindfulness, we are making peace with ourselves. The work you do on your yoga mat ripples throughout your life. Try not to pass judgment on your practice or criticize yourself. Try to go "opinion free" during your time on the mat.

Intention Five

Right Attitude: Everything Is Mind

SEAN

What We Think, We Become

Our thoughts can be like tiny gremlins talking incessantly inside our heads. We have 50,000 conversations each day with ourselves, some studies say. If my math is correct, that would be 2,000 discussions each hour, 34 little self-talks each minute. Every two seconds, we are blabbing to ourselves about something! What's worse, most of this stuff is just us replaying our insecurities and doubts. It's been found that 80% of what goes on in our heads is us questioning, judging, criticizing, and sometimes condemning ourselves.

A NATIVE AMERICAN LEGEND

A Grandfather from the Cherokee Nation was talking with his grandson about how he felt. He said, "I feel as if I have two wolves fighting inside of me. One wolf is the vengeful, angry, violent one. The other wolf is the loving, compassionate one."

The grandson asked, "Which wolf will win the fight inside of you?"

The grandfather answered, "The one I feed."

Negative thoughts are like bad wolves. If you feed them, they will grow and win. Listen to the conversations in your head. Do you hear a pattern forming? It might go something like this: my life stinks, bad things always happen to me, woe is me. That's OK. We are all aware, or at least we suspect, that this kind

> Attitude is a little thing that makes a big difference.
>
> WINSTON CHURCHILL

> Everything you are against weakens you. Everything you are for empowers you.
>
> WAYNE DYER

of negative self-talk influences our actions. As Albert Einstein said, "Weakness of attitude becomes weakness of character." Negative thoughts lead to negative action, or in some cases, to no action at all.

This Dyer quote is true because like attracts like. Whatever we direct our energy toward, we end up inviting into our lives. Other people pick up on our negative thoughts, and soon we are surrounded by people with the same destructive conversations in their heads. In this way, limiting thoughts, quite literally, limits our reality.

So what can we do? We begin by turning away from the bad wolf. Once you become aware of a critical or judgmental thought, simply notice it. It will take time. Don't get upset or frustrated if negative thoughts still keep popping up in your head. The first step is just noticing them and congratulating yourself for taking this first, big step. Eventually, you will learn to replace the bad wolves with good ones.

We can talk ourselves into or out of anything. During my first stint in the NFL, I was trying out for the Detroit Lions. They stick you with a roommate at the Holiday Inn in Pontiac, and I was very fortunate to room with a guy named Mike. He had an incredibly positive outlook. Each night we would sit in the room and talk about how lucky we were to be in the NFL. He was a rookie from Michigan State and I was a rookie from Pitt. The conversations were almost always positive—we talked about our supportive girlfriends, our supportive families, and our admiration of the coaches.

Most NFL players dread training camp for obvious reasons: it's monotonous, it's grueling, and you can be cut on a moment's notice. Oh yeah, and the food sucks. So having an upbeat roommate is a great bonus. And our positive attitudes translated into good performances. I was able to go toe-to-toe with the current Lions kicker, Jason Hanson. There were even days when I outperformed him. Mike made the team and went on to have a four-year career with Detroit and then Miami.

My next two NFL training camps were strikingly different. The next summer, I tried it with the Colts and had a roommate who spent every night wallowing on the phone with the girlfriend that he missed dearly. He moaned each day about how training camp was the pits. It was challenging to stay positive, and I found myself falling into his negativity.

Things can always be worse. I should have been happy with my crying roommate because the following year presented me with a roommate who was the world's loudest snorer. To top it off, he was a Penn State alum, and I was a Pitt alum. I slept on the ceramic tile bathroom floor.

> The only people who find what they are looking for in life are the fault finders.
>
> **FOSTER'S LAW**

Self-Esteem

It's been posited by the medical community that stress might be a culprit in 80% of all illnesses. Behind stress is low self-esteem. People with low self-esteem tend to find themselves in unsatisfying jobs and poor relationships. When we lack self-esteem, we don't spend time working on our spiritual and self-development because we feel we aren't worth the time and effort; our lives feel like a burden and we see ourselves as victims. We end a relationship and it's the other person's fault. We lose our job and it's the company's fault, and so on.

When we have high levels of self-esteem, on the other hand, we welcome the challenge of making ourselves better people: physically, mentally, emotionally, and spiritually. And yes, people with high self-esteem tend to be more successful in their careers and in their personal relationships. When we have high self-esteem, we look forward to the work ahead, rather than complaining about how long it will take. And here's the good news—being self-confident and full of self-esteem is a conscious decision you can make.

Your relationship with yourself is the most important relationship you will ever have. Being secure and strong with who you are makes you immune to the negative words and feelings of other people, and it

> The greatest discovery of my generation is that a human being can alter his life by altering his attitudes.
>
> **WILLIAM JAMES**

> The mind is everything. What you think, you become.
>
> **BUDDHA**

protects you from your own self-limiting thoughts. Building strong self-esteem begins by loving and believing in yourself. We must learn to love ourselves if we expect to love others. By improving our self-esteem, our relationships will improve as well.

Having a good relationship with yourself leads you to take full responsibility for your own thoughts and actions because the only judge is you. You become an independent person, freed from seeking approval from others. Our past events and circumstances do not shape us—how we interpret those experiences are what matter. So place a high value on yourself—this is crucial to becoming free. This self-confidence is not something we possess naturally but something we create and nurture. By practicing self-love and living with good self-esteem, we experience health and happiness. Take your current strengths and build on them.

Body Image

These days, we can't hide from the sculpted bodies on magazine covers. If we maintain wrinkles, crow's feet, cellulite, or any imperfections at all, we are considered flawed and inadequate. How did we all fall for this?

Many of us work out incessantly. We become neurotic about what we put into our bodies. This destructive behavior takes us over: body, mind and heart. It consumes us. There will always be someone skinnier, there will always be someone with a smaller ass. For a variety of reasons, we have been conditioned to compare and contrast ourselves with others.

A student in one of my classes was clearly struggling, taking numerous child's poses. After class, she approached me and asked if it was normal to feel nauseous while practicing yoga. It's actually quite rare. I asked her what she did before yoga. She said she had run six miles earlier that day. That explained it. It wasn't the yoga making her nauseous, it was the overtraining, taxing her body until she felt ill. Sure, professional athletes spend hours training. But why do people with families and regular jobs do this?

These thoughts are self-limiting, preventing us from experiencing happiness, confidence peace, and balance. Some people go to yoga expecting to find enlightenment, and in doing so, miss the joy of what is happening right at that moment. Instead of focusing on that imagined, perfect body, we need to focus on who we are. Instead of searching, we can find power and peace right where we are.

We must invert our thought processes, flip them upside down. Committing to positive thoughts, we take the first step towards happiness, health, and peace. We can spend our time obsessing over our thighs, or, cherishing our time with others. Feeling good is better than looking good. We need to give up our fixation on vanity. This is the key to a balanced life, and when we work from a place that is balanced, we open our hearts and minds to something bigger than ourselves. A new perspective that allows us to connect to our truth.

There is an ancient Chinese story of a farmer who owned an old horse that tilled his fields. One day, the horse escaped into the hills and when the farmer's neighbors sympathized with the old man over his bad luck, the farmer replied, "Bad luck? Good luck? Who knows?"

A week later, the horse returned with a herd of horses from the hills and this time the neighbors congratulated the farmer on his good luck. His reply was, "Good luck? Bad luck? Who knows?"

Then, when the farmer's son was attempting to tame one of the wild horses, he fell off its back and broke his leg. Everyone thought this was bad luck. Not the farmer, whose only reaction was, "Bad luck? Good luck? Who knows?"

Some weeks later, the army marched into the village and conscripted every able-bodied youth they found

If you don't like something, change it; if you can't change it, change the way you think about it.

MARY ENGELBREIT

The Kingdom of Heaven is not a place, but a state of mind.

JOHN BURROUGHS

there. When they saw the farmer's son with his broken leg, they let him off. Once again, the farmer's only reaction was, "Good luck? Bad luck? Who knows?"

Combine a positive attitude with balance. Stay cool, yet be determined. Be strong, yet easeful. Combine effort with rest. Try not to get too high and try not to get to down on yourself. Many of us live a life staying connected with only the extremes. It is up to us to be happy or to be miserable. Try not to look for a reason to be angry or offended. Many of us fall into this trap on a daily basis. By waking up and savoring every moment, we reconnect with our true selves. A good life or a bad life, you choose.

ATTITUDE

The longer I live, the more I realize the impact of attitude on life. Attitude, to me, is more important than facts. It is more important than the past, than education, than money, than circumstances, than failures, than successes, than what other people think or say or do. It is more important than appearance, giftedness or skill. It will make or break a company...a church...a home. The remarkable thing is, we have a choice every day regarding the attitude we will embrace for that day. We cannot change our past...we cannot change the inevitable. The only thing we can do is play on the one string we have, and that is our attitude...I am convinced that life is 10% what happens to me and 90% how I react to it. And so it is with you...we are in charge of our attitudes."

—Charles Swindoll

Do you know how well your yoga practice is working for you?

It seems as if some students have it figured out. They walk in with a smile, they smile in a Warrior 2, and they walk out with a smile.

Yoga will allow you to practice being calm in a difficult or stressful moment. The source of our problems doesn't have quite as much to do with the outside world as we might imagine. It's more likely to be our reaction and interpretation of any given situation that will dictate the nature of our experience. The external factors in life we have no control over, but we do have control over how we react to them. Frustration is an emotion that we control. We have no control over the external events in life, only how we react to them. In yoga, it's about struggling with something simple—can you be ok with it? It's like practicing in the shallow water of life. Take care of the inside.

In yoga, we practice "going with the flow." It means coming to accept and understand that we don't control every part of our lives at all times. Instead, we use our inner power to guide us. It is a mammoth leap of faith. It means that we accept the ups and downs of being human. It means putting trust that everything is being taken care of by God or spirits or whomever you honor, and believing that in the end it works out for our good.

The 92-year-old, petite, well-poised and proud lady, who is fully dressed each morning by eight o'clock, with her hair fashionably coiffed and makeup perfectly applied, even though she is legally blind, moved to a nursing home today. Her husband of 70 years recently passed away, making the move necessary. After many hours of waiting patiently in the lobby of the nursing home, she smiled sweetly when told her room was ready. As she maneuvered her walker to the elevator, I provided a visual description of her tiny room, including the eyelet sheets that had been hung on her window.

"I love it," she stated with the enthusiasm of an eight-year-old having just been presented with a new puppy.

"Mrs. Jones, you haven't seen the room....just wait."

"That doesn't have anything to do with it," she replied.

A yoga class in New York City:
   $20
Stainless steel water bottle:
   $25
Yoga pants that make your ass look small:
   $118
Being calm in a difficult moment:
   Priceless

Our attitude toward life determines life's attitude toward us.

JOHN MITCHELL

There are only two ways to live your life. One is, as though nothing is a miracle. The other is, as though everything is a miracle.

ALBERT EINSTEIN

"Happiness is something you decide on ahead of time. Whether I like my room or not doesn't depend on how the furniture is arranged; it's how I arrange my mind. I already decided to love it. It's a decision I make every morning when I wake up. I have a choice; I can spend the day in bed recounting the difficulty I have with the parts of my body that no longer work, or get out of bed and be thankful for the ones that do. Each day is a gift, and as long as my eyes open I'll focus on the new day and all the happy memories I've stored away...just for this time in my life."

Sean's Amazing Yoga Tips for Practicing the Right Attitude on Your Mat

Yoga imitates life—sometimes it will be hard, sometimes it will be easy. When that little voice of doubt starts talking, notice it and then try to move past it. Listen to your intuition and your spirit, for something greater than yourself to speak to you. After all, yoga allows us to face our fears in a safe environment.

Yoga poses can reveal your strengths and weaknesses. Some students make up their mind in the first 5 minutes of class that they already dislike yoga. They let their mind defeat them. They go right into judgment mode. This pose is awful. It's too hard. I can't hold it much longer, they think, tapping right into their inner dialogue of fear and doubt. Eventually, though, you learn how to approach a challenging moment on your mat. You find that while a pose may be uncomfortable, if you relax your mind it might feel really good or, at the very least, you can be okay in it. You may even discover that the poses you like the least, you need the most. Notice and recognize the difference between sensation and irritation. Don't forget—part of yoga is challenge. Sensations come up and we can feed them or starve them. During difficult moments remember, this is what you came for.

Intention Six

Embracing Change: Create Yourself

KAREN

We are often asked how we want to make a living but not how we want to live, what we want to create or build. My first yoga workshop was an experience I never anticipated. The practice focused on the quality of our minds and hearts, and I realized I hadn't asked myself these kinds of questions in a long time. I also knew no one could give me the answers I was seeking. There was no manual I could read, no degree I could earn. Yet I was so used to letting others guide me that I had given up listening to myself. I no longer trusted myself to make that big decision. What yoga gave me that weekend were tools—tools I could use to build the life I wanted. The answers would come from me. I would create my own path.

As I learn about my own growth, I share it with others. So often people say, "I feel like you were talking to me today when you were teaching." The truth is, I was talking about myself or an experience I had, but we all have similar experiences. The nature of being human is that we can relate to one another's feelings of panic, confusion and frustration, as well as our delight, joy and peacefulness. Yoga offers the gift of humanity and the opportunity to connect.

THE STORY OF THE BUTTERFLY

A man found the cocoon of a butterfly. One day a small opening appeared.

He sat and watched the butterfly for several hours as it struggled to squeeze its body through the tiny hole.

> When the winds of change blow we can build walls or make windmills.
>
> **CHINESE PROVERB**

Then it stopped, as if it couldn't go further. So the man decided to help the butterfly. He took a pair of scissors and snipped off the remaining bits of cocoon. The butterfly emerged easily but it had a swollen body and shriveled wings.

The man continued to watch it, expecting that any minute the wings would enlarge and expand enough to support the body. Neither happened. In fact, the butterfly spent the rest of its life crawling around. It was never able to fly. What the man in his kindness and haste did not understand: the restricting cocoon and the struggle required by the butterfly to get through the opening was a way of forcing the fluid from the body into the wings so that it would be ready for flight.

Sometimes struggles are exactly what we need in our lives. Going through life with no obstacles would cripple us. We would not be as strong as we could have been and we would never fly.

Life is full of bumps and bruises. We hold onto a vision of how things are supposed to be, and when life doesn't go as planned, we lose faith that life is not working out. Yet what makes us perfect is the ability to grow. Our imperfections let us know we are participating actively in our own lives.

The oyster, a symbol of compassion, creates a pearl out of dirt and sand. We don't need to throw out the bad and start over. We can embrace our imperfections—they are part of who we are they make us unique. When we work with our own insecurities with attention and love, we, too, can shine bright. We just have to remember to breathe.

A new teacher recently asked me how she could help students who seem uncomfortable in yoga. They strain and struggle, and the only break they take is to send a quick text under their mats. This is something I've seen many times—it's human nature to resist. It's not that people don't want to relax, it's that they don't know how. The word "relax" isn't part of their vocabulary yet. Luckily for us, our minds are hardwired to experience bliss—though turning purple, pushing and straining, will not lead you there (unless, of course, you are in labor!).When we move with compassion into whatever is blocking our path, we find the obstacles begin to soften.

Many of us struggle to be still and calm. When things get uncomfortable our first reaction is to dart. This is one of the hardest things we confront. We call this the flight, fight or surrender response. We can fight our way through the difficulties, we can check out and abandon the difficulties, or ideally, we can surrender and relax into it. We are working always towards surrender, giving up the fight because fighting just creates more tension and angst. Change is scary and very uncomfortable, but when we find ourselves in this place of challenge, we find that there is so much power in staying. Staying and breathing. In yoga, we call this your "center." It's your place of calmness and strength.

Off the coast of Maine, a Navy ship was sailing in a very dense fog. This night, the midshipman saw a fixed light in the distance and immediately contacted his captain.

"There's a light in the distance heading straight for us, what do you want me to do?"

The captain told him to flash a signal to the vessel, directing it to change course.

The vessel signaled back, "No, you change your course." Again the captain instructed the midshipman to command the oncoming vessel to change its course immediately.

Again the reply was, "No, you change your course."

With one last attempt, the midshipman signaled the vessel saying, "This is the Captain of a U.S. Navy battleship: change your course immediately."

The reply was, "No, you change your course. This is a lighthouse."

> Life is not about finding yourself, life is about creating yourself.
>
> GEORGE BERNARD SHAW

> With unfailing kindness, your life always presents what you need to learn. Whether you stay home or work in an office or whatever, the next teacher is going to pop right up.
>
> CHARLOTTE BECK

This is the typical way most of us deal with challenging situations. We want control over everything. We want the circumstances or events to change their course. If we work on changing our thoughts and ourselves then our lives can change.

Often the word "change" makes us anxious even though we all know that it is an essential element of life. Yet we almost instinctively resist it. Part of the process of change for me is asking for a little grace and having faith. Yoga is a place to be myself, to watch my thoughts and notice my dreams slip in. I feel relief from my day and consider how I can be a better parent. I think of ways to be more honest. I notice when I start to judge, when I start to compete. I try to be more gentle, more grateful and less judgmental. Yoga is perspective. Yoga is grace.

Each of us is unique on this planet. We are all here for a reason at this time. We all have gifts to offer this world at this time. It is our own individuality that allows us to make a difference. I know there are times when we are overwhelmed by smallness, when thinking about change is for other people. We get lulled to sleep by our daily activities and just go through the motions.

Then something comes along as a wake-up call. A time when we realize that life is moving fast, much faster than we would like. This is why birthdays are good—they are reminders to celebrate ourselves. They give us time to reflect and in these moments of reflection we are pressed to make an imprint on this world. When did you stop celebrating yourself?

We live in a world where communication is instant and accessible, yet we often feel isolated. We are afraid of being alone or losing people close to us and it is so easy to stay contracted, just waiting for a tragedy to steal our happiness. It's hard to be a light in the middle of an ocean—you get put out fast. We need to make the choice to be connected, to surround ourselves with positive people. This is why we have to ask, "How is my yoga practice going to make me a better person today?"

One of the most satisfying aspects of owning a yoga studio is watching the community evolve—friendships blossom, relationships grow. Simply observing this brings joy to peoples' lives. New students come to the studio intimidated and nervous, and then they see students talking to one another, hugging and catching up. They feel the healthy vibe, that we are a community of like-minded people. This commonality spreads and empowers people to ask more of themselves to make positive change in the world around them.

As yoga students, we are part of long lineage—a 5,000-year-old tradition that is designed to take us to new places physically, emotionally and spiritually. In its earliest origins, yoga was never designed to be easy. Yoga is hard. But through patience and working on what we need to work on, there is progress. We practice forgiving ourselves so we can forgive others. We practice being gentle on ourselves so we can in turn be gentle with others. We are good to ourselves so that we can practice patience and love, so that we can be of service to the world. For, as Buddhists say, "At the end of the day, all we own are our actions." We come together as many flames and generate a big light.

A STUDENT'S STORY

My journey with Amazing Yoga began when I walked through the doors of the Wexford studio a dangerously overweight smoker. A year before my wedding date, I had made the decision to try and get healthy. It was not an easy decision to make, but I know now that I had decided that day to live rather than continue to hide. As I had so many times in the past, I walked into class terrified and anticipating failure.

What happened to me over the next year was purely amazing, no pun intended. With the support of fantastic teachers, I learned to look inside myself and find my inner strength. They enabled me to believe that I could do this. They encouraged me to be the best that I could be and to always "breathe" through the difficult

> Never doubt that a small group of thoughtful people could change the world. Indeed, it's the only thing that ever has.
>
> **MARGARET MEAD**

> God give me the grace to accept things I cannot change;
> the courage to change the things I can change,
> and the wisdom to know the difference.
>
> **THE SERENITY PRAYER**

times in my life. They reminded me at each practice that I did have the strength to succeed.

Today I am 60 pounds lighter, smoke-free for over a year, and practicing yoga 3-4 times a week. My wedding was wonderful. I am so thankful I found yoga and through my practice gained power over my life again. Once the unhealthy overweight girl, I am now challenging myself each and every day, not only in my yoga practice but through other adventures, including running a 5K race. None of my happiness and renewed appreciation for my health or my life would have been possible without the strength, support, and truly amazing moments that happened through yoga.

--Crystal

Life is constantly changing and so are we. We need to learn to adapt. The one aspect of parenting that reveals itself to me daily is the need to adapt. I can plan and map out all the details and think I have the situation covered and of course, inevitably, something happens that I did not anticipate. When unanticipated changes happen, we need to adapt and discover what changes seem healthy and feel right and which ones might not work. This is the art of being flexible.

The most valuable quality you can ever develop to deal with change is flexibility. Keeping an open mind and being adaptable when things go wrong, as they often do, instead of becoming frustrated and upset is how we stay open to all of the possibilities.

In ancient times, a King had a boulder placed on a roadway. Then, he hid himself and watched to see if anyone would remove the huge rock. Some of the king's wealthiest merchants and courtiers came by and simply walked around it. Many loudly blamed the King for not keeping the roads clear, but none did anything about getting the stone out of the way. Then, a peasant came along carrying a load of vegetables. Upon approaching the boulder, the peasant laid down

---

Challenges are what make life interesting; overcoming them is what makes life meaningful.

JOSHUA MARINE

his burden and tried to move the stone to the side of the road. After much pushing and straining, he finally succeeded. After the peasant picked up his load of vegetables, he noticed a purse lying in the road where the boulder had been. The purse contained many gold coins and a note from the King indicating that the gold was for the person who removed the boulder from the roadway.

The peasant learned what many of us never understand. Every obstacle presents an opportunity to improve our condition.

Karen's Amazing Yoga Tips for Practicing Change on Your Mat

I am reminded in my daily practice just how challenging and uncomfortable certain poses can be. Our mat becomes a training ground for our life outside of yoga, so watch how the breath shortens and the jaw tightens and the mind races with panic. When that happens, breathe a little deeper. Let the winds of change move through you so you can relax instead of resisting. It's been said that yoga is a 70-year process. Be patient with yourself. Challenge yourself but at the same time take care of yourself. Sensations will come up in yoga: be sure that the physical sensations are not pain. Of course if they *are* pain, back off. But if they are just strong healthy sensations, this is where the work is. B.K.S. Iyengar said, "The pose begins when you want to come out of it." Albert Einstein said, "In the middle of difficulty lies opportunity." The opportunity for change can be found in this place of discomfort.

Intention Seven

Letting Go: It Leads to Freedom

SEAN

We create our own suffering. When we let go, we rid ourselves of suffering. We need to let go of the stuff that is in our way, the stuff holding us back. Stuff like guilt, resentment, obsessing over our bodies, abusive relationships, money, status, fear, doubts, worry, harsh judgments of ourselves and others. Holding on to things is like being stuck in a bad relationship, one that we know isn't good for us, for both our growth and happiness. But we're stubborn, we tighten our grip and end up suffering needlessly.

Letting go does not mean giving up or quitting. Letting go means connecting to your inner wisdom. There is a story about how African hunters catch monkeys. It can be very difficult to corral these intelligent creatures, so hunters invented a method to entice them. A small jar containing nuts is placed at the base of a tree. The opening of the jar is wide enough to allow the monkey to reach in, but when he tries to withdraw his hand, full of nuts, he is unable to do so. To free his hand, the monkey must let go of the nuts, but many stay there, trapped by their full hand, until the hunter returns.

We can all think of ways we trap ourselves, hold ourselves back because we are too stubborn to open our hand. Freedom comes when we let go.

Old Habits Die Hard

Once, during a teacher training in Mexico, a participant spoke about her bad luck with guys. Day after

> When one door of happiness closes, another opens; but often we look so long at the closed door that we do not see the one which has been opened for us.
>
> **HELEN KELLER**

day, she told us how they treated her horribly, and how she would stick around long after she came to this realization. Afraid to move on, she thought she considered herself unworthy, unlovable.

A big iguana lived in the yoga room that year. Each day, the iguana perched on the same beam above the class, and each day the woman set up her mat directly beneath it. Each day, the iguana shit on her. Then one day, the woman moved her mat.

"If you keep saying things are going to be bad," Isaac Bashevis Singer wrote, "you have a good chance of being a prophet."

Many of us believe we cannot help the way we are, but this is not true. Sure, we cannot change the past, but by staying with old habits, we make it impossible to experience new results. The past is simply the past—it exists only in our minds. We decide whether to repeat the same mistakes or take our lives in a new direction. The past affects us only if we give it the power to do so. We are in command of our lives.

There is a famous Zen story about two monks who had taken vows not to associate with women.

While out walking one day, they came to a river that had to be forded. A woman on the bank needed to cross as well but couldn't do it by herself. One of the monks carried her across on his back. Once on the other side, he put her down and the two monks resumed their journey.

After about ten miles, the other monk finally spoke, saying angrily, "You shouldn't have carried that woman." The first monk just smiled and said, "I put her down ten miles ago. Why are you still carrying her?"

When these doors slam on us, why do we stare at them for so long? When I was playing football for the Detroit Lions, one of my coaches, the late Frank

> If it seems like everything is coming at you, maybe you are in the wrong lane.
>
> **ANONYMOUS**

> **Other people do not have to change for us to experience peace of mind.**
>
> GERALD JAMPOLSKY

Ganz, would motivate us with inspirational quotes and tidbits. One night during training camp, he told us at a meeting, "Hey boys, you must expect the unexpected at all times." He must have been talking to me, because the next day I got cut from the team, and I certainly didn't expect that at the time. But isn't that the truth? Who knows what awaits us around the corner. But when I got cut, I went into a standstill and struggled to move forward, not seeing the opportunity to learn from the experience.

By letting go of our past heartaches and failures, we ensure ourselves a bright future. Unfortunately for many of us, too often we stay attached to the past, or to just what we are familiar with. We end up missing the opportunities right in front of us. Challenges may arise or doors may close, but the number of other doors available to us is infinite. Life is filled with wins and losses, problems come up at work and at home. We have very little control of these events, but we can control how we react to them. By shifting our attention to the open doors, we are pleasantly surprised at the possibilities. It is not so easy letting go of our attachments to the familiar, letting go our fear of the unknown. Yet when we keep our focus on the open doors, we live a life of freedom that always moves forward spiritually.

Our deepest fear is not that we are inadequate. Our deepest fear is that we are powerful beyond measure. It is our light, not our darkness that most frightens us. We ask ourselves,Who am I to be brilliant, gorgeous, talented, fabulous? Actually, who are you not to be?

You are a child of God. Your playing small does not serve the world. There's nothing enlightened about shrinking so that other people won't feel insecure around you. We are all meant to shine as children do. We were born to make manifest the glory of God that is w hin us. It's not just in some of us; it's in everyone. And as we let our own light shine,we unconsciously give other people permission to do the same. As we're liberated from our own fear, our presence automatically liberates others.

—Marianne Williamson

Fear has a way of stopping us in life. It could be fear of failing, fear of success, fear of screwing up, or fear of what others think of us. We can spend a lifetime second guessing ourselves over and over. We end up missing out on life by standing on the sidelines. We let ourselves be defeated by our internal conversations. Let go of fear. Surprisingly, when we do our best, most of the time it is much better than we think. And when we fall short or fail, these failures can be our greatest teachers in life. Recognize fear, but then let it go. If your intuition is telling you to go forward, listen to it.

Stop feelings of guilt and resentment. Many times our feelings of guilt have nothing to do with us and resentments get in the way of loving others. When we hold on to guilt and resentment, the only one who suffers is us.

"Because he didn't love me, no one can love me."

"Because I was abandoned, others will abandon me."

"My life sucked as a kid, therefore my life will suck as an adult."

Only when we let go of these stories, can we move forward and become free.

We all experience hurt when our needs or expectations are not met. By refusing to forgive, we imagine it gives us the upper hand. We think that by forgiving we condone the other person's words or actions. We find ways, in other words, to justify our hurt and anger. We use the pain we feel as an excuse, identifying with it until we are just a collection of hurts.

Learn to forgive yourself and others. By forgiving, we put the past where it belongs: in the past. By refusing to forgive, we may feel powerful and self-righteous, but again, who suffers most? We do. Our own personal

> Sometimes you have to let go to see if there was anything worth holding on to.
>
> **ANONYMOUS**

freedom is damaged. Our anger turns to sickness, to physical disease.

Of course, forgiving is often easier said than done; many of us carry grudges for our entire lives. Yet we can choose to learn from, rather than dwell on, the past. We can use challenges—hurts, misdeeds—to grow spiritually and emotionally. Forgiving is empowering. By the same token, don't spend your time feeling wronged, waiting around for others to apologize to you. We imprison ourselves by holding on to grudges and waste our precious time on earth.

When we let go, we raise our level of consciousness. Albert Einstein said that we cannot solve a problem at the same level of consciousness that gave rise to the problem. When we heap the blame on others, we live in the world as victims and stay stuck. But when we decide to take responsibility for our own feelings, we alter our consciousness; and in this way, we take a big step toward healing. Love is the end result of letting go. When we let go, we experience love and transformation. We experience happiness.

A story tells of a merchant in a small town who had identical twin sons. The boys worked for their father in the department store he owned and, when he died, they took over the store. Everything went well until the day a dollar bill disappeared. One of the brothers had left the bill on the cash register and walked outside with a customer. When he returned, the money was gone.

He asked his brother, "Did you see that dollar bill on the cash register?" His brother replied that he had not. But the young man kept probing and questioning. He would not let it alone. "Dollar bills just don't get up and walk away! Surely you must have seen it!"

There was subtle accusation in his voice. Tempers began to rise. Resentment set in. Before long, a deep and bitter chasm divided the young men. They refused to speak. They finally decided they could no longer work together and a dividing wall was built down the center of the store. For 20 years, hostility and bitterness grew, spreading to their families and to the community.

Then one day a man in an automobile licensed in another state stopped in front of the store. He walked in and asked the clerk, "How long have you been here?"

The clerk replied that he'd been there all his life. The customer said, "I must share something with you. 20 years ago I was riding the rails and came into this town in a boxcar. I hadn't eaten for three days. I came into this store from the back door and saw a dollar bill on the cash register. I put it in my pocket and walked out. All these years I haven't been able to forget that. I know it wasn't much money, but I had to come back and ask your forgiveness."

The stranger was amazed to see tears well up in the eyes of this middle-aged man. "Would you please go next door and tell that same story to the man in the store?" he said. Then the man was even more amazed to see two middle-aged men, who looked very much alike, embracing each other and weeping together in the front of the store.

After 20 years, the brokenness was mended. The wall of resentment that divided them came down.

A STUDENT'S STORY

As a kid, I felt too much of the happiness, anger, hope, and anxiety of other people. I learned to be tough, and so keep a little distance between myself and the world. As a young woman, that bravado turned into recklessness. A nurse friend tells me the addicts she works with often have little tolerance for pain. What might seem merely uncomfortable to many people, they find genuinely excruciating.

When I first started practicing at Amazing Yoga, I muscled my way though the classes. I loved the vigorous sun salutations, all that sweat. But holding poses was uncomfortable. I found the stillness frightening, weirdly painful. The first time I came into half-pigeon pose, I cried on my mat. I had no idea what was wrong. Utkatasana was also hard. The teacher would tell us it was like sitting in a chair, and all I could think was that this was the worst chair ever—I'd take this chair to the curb next garbage day. I hated this chair!

But as I kept practicing, something inside me began to loosen, to let go. One day, as we moved into utkatasana, I remembered sitting beside a lake where I'd first heard, and then seen, a big bird fishing, dropping into the water over and over again. With no urgency, just a patient, methodical release. I sat into the pose that afternoon, relaxed into the chair. Every day I do yoga, this is what I practice: letting go of fear, relaxing into my life, being okay feeling just what I feel.

--Jen

Sean's Amazing Yoga Tips for Practicing Letting Go on Your Mat

Letting go is difficult to do at times. We practice letting go in yoga by not holding our breath. We practice conscious breathing by allowing the breath to pass smoothly and freely in and out of our noses. When we focus on breathing, our body relaxes and releases, and soon the mind releases, too. Let go of old habits—over-thinking, over-planning, trying to control or fix things. Let go of trying to figure other people out. When attachments come up—like the fear of growing older, a lost love—let them go.

Focus instead on being completely present; let the pose be what it is. When you lose your balance, get back up and start again, releasing feelings of self-defeat. We are not performing—we are just practicing. Surrender to the pose by releasing extra effort or tension, both physical and mental. When we surrender in a yoga pose, we are not giving up—we are just relaxing in.

Intention Eight

Gratitude: The Most Difficult Arithmetic to Master

People usually consider walking on water
or in thin air a miracle.
But I think the real miracle
is not to walk either on water or in thin air,
but to walk on earth.
Every day we are engaged in a miracle
which we don't even recognize:
a blue sky, white clouds, green leaves,
the black, curious eyes of a child—
our own two eyes.
All is a miracle.

—Thich Nhat Hanh, "Miracle of Mindfulness"

When we were young, Sean and I had incredible wanderlust. We dreamed about the perfect place to live and raise our children. "This city will have culture," we said, or, "If we move here, we can get outside." In ten years, it seemed like we moved ten times. Finally, we understood that happiness doesn't exist in any one city. We realized that what we were looking for wasn't a place on a map.

We all do this. We all think "Someday I will find the ideal mate, someday I will have kids, someday when I have the money, when I finish school…" But when the focus is on the someday, we miss out on the real juice of life, the real magic of today. Once, when I had a long day of teaching ahead of me, I thought to myself, "I can't wait for this day to be over." How easy

> The most difficult arithmetic to master is the art of counting our blessings.
>
> UNKNOWN

> Beyond a wholesome discipline,
> be gentle with yourself.
> You are a child of the universe no less than the trees and the stars;
> you have a right to be here.
> And whether or not it is clear to you, no doubt the universe is unfolding as it should.
>
> **DESIDERATA**

it is to want the next thing. There I was in a room full of students who had given me the chance to share myself with them. In turn, they would leave the class feeling better, and be more available to others. Yet I was wishing my life away, all those precious hours of opportunity. At that moment, I realized that it was my obligation to show up for my students and for myself, for the life I had created. Feeling grateful is the key to good health. Being able to see what's valuable in our everyday lives is essential to happiness. I have never wished a day away since then.

When I first started doing yoga, I was so competitive. My whole life had been based on how I could perform. Dance, sports, grades. At some point, I realized the pressure to "be better" was bringing me more discomfort than satisfaction. Yoga began to teach me that comparing myself to others, looking "out there," was not giving me the answers I sought.

I see this ambition in yoga students. "The day I get crow pose, I will be…"

But the joy of yoga is not straining to get somewhere. Yoga is about being where you are and breathing. Being more flexible or stronger or more graceful in a posture doesn't make you a healthier person. There will always be someone more flexible, smarter and skinnier, so we need to learn to focus on our own individual strengths and healthfully improve ourselves however we can.

We see people come into their genius, their power and strength, but they are not better than anyone else. They just listen to that small voice called intuition. They let perspective and compassion replace demands and judgments. Gratitude is the key to unlocking positive energy in our lives. All of the great people in history—Jesus, Mother Theresa, Buddha, Gandhi, Mohammed—speak of gratitude, of gentleness and loving others. As you consider how you can be kinder, more thankful for your life, your yoga mat becomes your own kingdom, a place where you can understand and love yourself better. It becomes a platform for self-discovery.

When we lived in Seattle, we took daily walks along Puget Sound. Usually, we had a clear view of Mt. Rainier. It was such a huge presence, and yet seemed so close you felt as though you could walk right into it. There were days, though, when clouds moved in and the mountain would simply disappear. It amazed me the way we suddenly couldn't see this magnificent volcano right there in front of our eyes, that we couldn't even imagine what was on the other side of those clouds.

How easily we lose track of wonder. Consider the way excuses become clouds that obscure what we think possible.

"I can't do yoga because I am not flexible."
"I can't do yoga because I am not good at it."

Yoga is about feeling good where we are, but it is also about showing up, with faith and grace, for those daily walks. Yoga is about perspective. Sure weather moves in, but the mountain will reveal itself again. It always does.

Knowing others is intelligence. Knowing yourself is true wisdom.

LAO TSU

Once there was a doctor who won international acclaim for some medicines that he discovered. Everyone spoke about his intelligence, sincerity and contribution to society. In an interview, he was asked who the people behind his success were. He suddenly remembered a teacher from his primary school.

She had given him tremendous love and support at the time when he was going through a tough phase. His parents had just divorced and the teacher had made it her personal responsibility to give him an extra smile, a nudge, a pat, and a hug whenever he passed by. Her love had carried him through and ensured that he became a class topper rather than a slacker. He went back to his school to thank his teacher but found that she had moved to another city. Taking her recent address from the records, he wrote her a long letter thanking her for being there just when he needed her.

> *To be upset over what you don't have is to waste what you do have.*
>
> **KEN S. KEYES, JR.**

He had tears in his eyes as he remembered her kind smile and warm eyes. In just a few days, he heard from his teacher. She wrote, "In the 50 years that I worked in that school as a primary teacher, you are the first student who has remembered me and thanked me. I am now 80 years old and very ill. Your single letter has made my entire lifetime's efforts worth it. Thank you, for thanking me and making me realize that my life was not a waste." The student clutched the letter to his heart and wept. Indeed, gratitude is a beautiful feeling, for the one who is feeling it and the one to whom the gratitude is felt. Let us say thank you more often, to more people.

Relationships, gratitude, compassion and love you can trust—these traits promote true lasting happiness. We all know that our new iPhone, or addition on the house will not provide us with lasting happiness yet we continue to seek material possessions to feel fulfilled. Whenever researchers perform studies of the happiest countries, despite being one of the most affluent countries in the world, we generally do not fare well. It seems to be part of human nature to always want more. In yoga, its poses or a white light beaming through our bodies, or maybe even balanced chakras, yet we are living and that is a miracle. Let us recognize the miracle that is happening right in this moment.

Expressing gratitude is transformative, just as transformative as expressing complaint. Imagine an experiment involving two people. One is asked to spend ten minutes each morning and evening expressing gratitude (there is always something to be grateful for), while the other is asked to spend the same amount of time practicing complaining (there is, after all, always something to complain about). One of the subjects is saying things like, "I hate my job. I can't stand this apartment. Why can't I make enough money? My spouse doesn't get along with me. That dog next door never stops barking and I just can't stand this neighborhood." The other is saying things like, "I'm really grateful for the opportunity to work; there are so many people these days who can't even find a job. And I'm sure grateful for my health. What a gorgeous day; I really like this fall breeze." They do this experiment for a year. Guaranteed, at the end of that year the person practicing complaining will have deeply reaffirmed all his negative "stuff" rather than having let it go, while the one practicing gratitude will be a very grateful person...Expressing gratitude can, indeed, change our way of seeing ourselves and the world.

—Roshi John Daido Loori

One day a father and his rich family took his young son on a trip to the country with the firm purpose to show him how poor people can be. They spent a day and a night in the farm of a very poor family. When they got back from their trip the father asked his son, "How was the trip?"

"Very good, Dad!"

"Did you see how poor people can be?" the father asked.

"Yeah!"

"And what did you learn?"

The son answered, "I saw that we have a dog at home, and they have four. We have a pool that reaches to the middle of the garden, they have a creek that has no end. We have imported lamps in the garden, they have the stars. Our patio reaches to the front yard, they have a whole horizon."

When the little boy was finishing, his father was speechless.

His son added, "Thanks, Dad, for showing me how poor we are!"

Isn't it true that it all depends on the way you look at things? If you have love, friends, family, health, good

> I cried because I had no shoes, until I met a man who had no feet.
>
> **ANONYMOUS**

humor and a positive attitude toward life, you've got everything.

You can't buy any of these things. You can have all the material possessions you can imagine, provisions for the future, etc., but if you are poor of spirit, you have nothing.

Avoid self-pity. Recognize that everyone, even pop stars and millionaires, have problems. Accept your situation and take small steps to improve it. Helping others in little ways brings unexpected happiness. It takes your focus away from the "Poor Me!" syndrome.

Appreciate and treasure what you have now. You can never tell what will happen tomorrow. You may lose that special friend or loved one whom you've been taking for granted.

> A wise man once said, "Seek not wealth or riches. Instead, seek to be wise."

Practicing gratitude goes hand-in-hand with yoga; they both cultivate awareness and mindfulness. Sure many of us are thankful for having the things we want in our life, like a loving family and health, but we all know how easy is it to lose sight of all the goodness in our lives when we lose something or our kids start screaming or we have a bad day. Being grateful is the first law of attraction and it is essential to your health and well-being. Being grateful turns bad things into good ones. It doesn't cost much money or require much time. It is just taking a few moments of your day to be grateful for the full spectrum of your life—the ups and downs, the high and the lows. Challenges create opportunities to promote growth and greatness. Challenges bring depth to our character and give us appreciation. If you spend time every day expressing gratitude in a way that is meaningful to you, it will quickly become an integral part of your life. Like any habit, the more we practice it, the more natural it becomes. Being grateful for the life you have created allows you to be truly alive.

BE THANKFUL

Be thankful that you don't already have everything you desire—
if you did, what would there be to look forward to?

Be thankful when you don't know something,
for it gives you the opportunity to learn.

Be thankful for the difficult times.
During those times you grow.

Be thankful for your limitations,
because they give you opportunities for improvement.

Be thankful for each new challenge,
because it will build your strength and character.

Be thankful for your mistakes.
They will teach you valuable lessons.

Be thankful when you're tired and weary,
because it means you've made a difference.

It is easy to be thankful for the good things.
A life of rich fulfillment comes to those who are
also thankful for the setbacks.

Gratitude can turn a negative into a positive.
Find a way to be thankful for your troubles,
and they can become your blessings.

—anonymous

When I first stepped into the studio, I was emotionally spent. Battling depression, I had lost my father suddenly to leukemia a few months earlier, a young cousin over Christmas to a drug overdose. I walked over to the teacher and explained that I had no yoga experience, that I had never stepped into a yoga studio in my life. She assured me that I would be fine, encouraged me to take rest and drink water as I needed to.

People were laughing and talking. Class was full, but nobody seemed to mind. People were rolling out their mats and relaxing. No one had phones out, no one was cussing or smoking, just happy chatter. The teacher was easygoing and friendly. She took her time to correct postures, even though the class was full. Although I was a bit intimidated—I didn't know any of the poses—I continued practicing with the rest of the class. As we moved through the poses, I felt myself struggling a bit, but I felt lighter emotionally. I felt a bit centered. I felt that my whole body and mind had opened up. I heard myself breathing through my nose.

I think it is no accident that I found yoga. I practice regularly now and I have never had a negative experience. Yoga truly welcomes everyone, all shapes and all colors. Now four months later, I participate in the studio's work exchange program at two different locations and I have lost several inches from my waistline. I ordered a dress online recently and had to send it back—too big, imagine that! Although I am still grieving the sudden loss of my dear father, I am grateful that I found such a positive atmosphere to practice in, to reach my highest potential.

—Rasheda

Karen's Amazing Yoga Tips for being Grateful on Your Mat

When you fall over or cannot keep your balance in a pose, notice what you say to yourself. Listen to your self-talk, your inner voice. If you are being critical, give yourself some love and compassion. Try to not make your yoga practice one more thing to strive for, one more way to compete with yourself or others. The poses are just vehicles to move us from where we are in this moment to where we could be. Ideally, they transport us from being critical of others and ourselves to a place of acceptance, a place where we can be grateful for the lives we have and the bodies that allow this physical practice. Remember that life is about doing your best with what you have, and part of being human is that we fall down. Instead of meeting ourselves with worry, with anger and frustration, let's practice getting back up with ease, faith, grace, and gratitude. Think about how lucky we are to be able to move our limbs. How blessed we are to be alive. Being alive is the greatest miracle.

Three

On Your Mat: Power Vinyasa Yoga Sequences

AMAZING yoga

We practice yoga to feel good, to connect with our true selves and ultimately, to become better people. We practice yoga to become stronger, more graceful, and balanced, to gain a greater sense of health and well-being. Practicing yoga produces incredible medical benefits: from fighting diseases like diabetes to reducing stress and obesity. The poses bring our bodies into harmony. Because ideally, we want to remain in this healthy body as long as possible so that we can do for others as long as possible.

YOGA BREATHING

Breath brings magic to your yoga practice! Yoga will make you flexible and strong, but the breath will take you deeper and allow you to tap into the potential of your body, mind, and spirit. Calm, steady breath flow is what connects you to the present moment, what sustains you through difficult moments. Breath brings us into balance, allows our inner body and soul to shine and radiate.

Breath is what makes yoga more than just exercise. But because we aren't used to thinking about our breath, this can be the most challenging part of yoga. So, before we dive into the poses, let's tackle the how of yoga breathing.

We practice *ujjayi* (ooh-jy-yee) breathing, a deep throat breathing that sounds like a whisper. Start by breathing in through your nose slowly, narrowing down your inhale and then your exhale, creating a soft noise in the back of your throat. The breath sounds a little like Darth Vader!

Your breath should be smooth, not choppy. But don't force it—breathing shouldn't increase your workload. The only thing that increases is your awareness of your breath.

Ujjayi breathing is a discipline. It allows you to take in enough oxygen and create enough energy to carry you through the entire class, while at the same time keeping your mind and attention on the present moment. By synchronizing our movements with the breath, they become one. We inhale on movements that open, such as sweeping up our arms or initiating a backbend. When we bend forward or close in a pose, we exhale. Another way to think about it is that when we expand we breathe in, when we contract we breathe out. Breathing this way allows us to flow from pose to pose with grace and a sense of ease. A complete yoga breath includes one inhale and one exhale; with the exception of final relaxation, we use *ujjayi* breathing the entire practice.

AVOID INJURIES—FIND THE YOGA "SWEET SPOT." IT'S PRETTY SWEET!

In yoga: **No Pain = No Pain.**

While injuries in yoga are rare, they can and do happen. When they occur, it's usually because a student tried to do too much, too fast and wasn't paying attention to what he or she was feeling. Never move quickly into or out of a pose. Avoid jamming your body into a pose or pushing yourself too hard. We want to work, but we need be sensitive to our bodies.

This is one of the great dichotomies of yoga: finding balance between strength and softness, pushing and relaxing, challenging yourself while being gentle with yourself. If we don't push ourselves hard enough, there will be little challenge for our bodies and minds. We want to feel some sensations in order to learn more about ourselves—how we react, how we judge ourselves, what our level of patience is. If we push ourselves too hard, we risk injury or at the very least experience unnecessary pain.

This magical place between too much and too little is known as "balance" or what some call the "yoga sweet spot". We stretch deeper incrementally, pausing at each threshold. We never muscle our way into a pose, never use brute force—it's more like softening in. When we go deeper, it should always feel natural, never forced. Let the breath guide you. If a pose doesn't feel right, it's not.

We've got some bad news and some good news. The bad news is, yoga never gets easy. The good news is, yoga never gets easy. It is always challenging—that's why yoga continually presents with opportunities for growth. But over time, we discover that we can approach our yoga with a greater sense of ease. Our yoga practice should be a celebration, it should be fun and joyous.

SOME THINGS TO KEEP IN MIND AS YOU PRACTICE

An important part of any yoga practice is "trial and error." When you come into a pose, feel free to be creative and experimental. Look at your yoga practice as a process and remember that the poses were not designed to stress you out. The old yogis didn't sit around 5,000 years ago thinking, "A-ha, now here's a good pose, this one will really piss off those Westerners someday! Their hips will scream on this one, ha-ha-ha!"

Not a single pose is worth getting angry or anxious about. And certainly, no pose is worth injury! Adjust your feet or your hands: these poses should be challenging, but you should never, ever feel pain. (*If it's pain, you must refrain! If it's discomfort, you must remain!*) Remain in the pose, that is, by **breathing** and relaxing as best you can!

Don't worry about mastering the poses or doing so called "advanced poses." Advanced poses to not equal advanced spirituality. Some students want to go from doing Child's Pose to standing on their heads in one week. They want to go from A to Z without all those pesky B's and Q's in between. If we approach our practice with this "more-is-better" mindset, we have completely missed what yoga is about. Enjoy the process!

OK, let's practice!

The following sequence takes 30 minutes. It's a great way to familiarize yourself with the poses without taking a huge chunk out of your day. Find a quiet place in your house. Roll out your mat and you're ready to go. You may find a yoga block and a towel useful as well. The practice starts slow with "Shifting Gears," then moves on to some warm-ups called Sun A's and Sun B's. For the meat of the practice, you can choose between The Power Sequence and The Strength Sequence. Next comes some brief Core Work. Finish your practice with The Cool Down.

Please note that while there are many ways to approach these poses, we list just a small handful of "tips" for each. Try out the Tips and see which ones work for you. Your body has an incredible ability to find its own way, to go deeper if it needs to. By the same token, be open to the Modifications when your body tells you to back off.

SHIFTING GEARS

We use these first few poses to settle into our bodies. As we focus on our breathing, we make a commitment to setting distractions aside and being fully present. We set an intention for ourselves, a simple reminder of why we came to our mats today, why we decided to practice yoga.

1. Child's Pose (relax here for at least three minutes)

2. Downward Facing Dog (take 10 deep breaths)

Transition: Walk to the front of your mat

3. Rag Doll (hold for 10 breaths)

Transition: Release the arms, bring the feet together, come up slow to standing

4. Mountain Pose

1. Child's Pose (Balasana)

(bah-LAHS-anna): *bala* = child

Child's Pose is a resting pose that can be taken before or after any pose, and is a great pose to begin your practice. Not only does it stretch the hips, thighs, and ankles, but it also calms the mind and relieves stress. **Spend at least three minutes** in this pose before moving into Downward Facing Dog. If at any time during your practice you feel overwhelmed, come back to Child's Pose. Appreciate the calmness and quiet it offers you.

TIPS

- *Spread the knees out hip-width or wider*
- *Big toes touch*
- *Arms extended out in front or along your sides*
- *Rest your forehead on the floor*
- *Begin to make the pose active by breathing in and out of your nose*

2. Downward Facing Dog (Adho Mukha Svanasana)

(AH-doh MOO-kah shvah-NAHS-anna)
mukha = face; *svana* = dog

We practice Downward Facing Dog many times during a class. It is both a resting and active pose, and is an incredible strength builder. Downward Facing Dog stretches your back muscles, broadens your chest, and increases upper body strength. It also stimulates the brain and nervous system. **Hold for 10 deep breaths.**

Modifications:

Bend your knees

TIPS

- Place the hands as flat as possible, shoulder-width distance apart
- Feet are hip-width distance apart and parallel
- Spread out the fingers and press into the knuckles
- Head and neck relaxed
- Press the thighs and hips back
- Heels press gently down towards the floor
- Tailbone towards the sky

3. Rag Doll (Uttanasana)

(OOT-tan-AHS-ahna)
ut = intense; *tan* = stretch

This pose naturally lengthens the spine and produces a feeling of relaxation. Rag Doll increases the flexibility of the lower back and the hamstrings. **Hold for 10 deep breaths.**

TIPS

- Place feet hip-width distance apart
- Grab opposite elbows
- Relax your head
- Hips move gently forward

Modifications:

Bend your knees

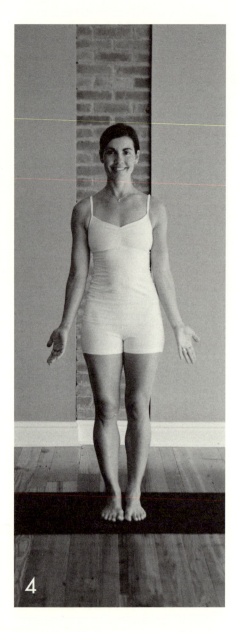

4. Mountain Pose (Tadasana)

(tah-DAHS-anna); *tada* = mountain

Mountain Pose brings the body into beautiful alignment. More active than it appears, Mountain Pose teaches us to maintain a graceful, yet easeful posture throughout our practice.

TIPS

- Feet together
- Chest open
- Shoulders relaxed
- The top of the head extends toward the ceiling
- Weight is even on both feet

WARM-UP SEQUENCE #1 (SUN SALUTATION A)

A classic warm-up sequence, Sun Salutation A mimics the qualities of the sun by building and radiating energy. Using both sides of the body equally, Sun A prepares our muscles and joints for the movements to come. It gets us breathing, matching our breath with movement. By moving in and out of simple postures like Mountain Pose and Downward Facing Dog, we establish flow and rhythm.

1. Mountain Pose

2. Forward Fold

3. Half-way Lift

4. High Push-Up

5. Low Push-Up

6. Upward Facing Dog

7. Downward Facing Dog (Hold for 5 breaths)

Transition: Between Sun A's:

   A. Walk or jump to your hands

   B. Halfway Lift (inhale)

   C. Forward Fold (exhale)

   D. Reach the arms to the sky and come into Mountain Pose

Repeat entire sequence 3-4 times

1. Mountain Pose

Begin in Mountain Pose. Reach your arms up to the sky and then bow forward.

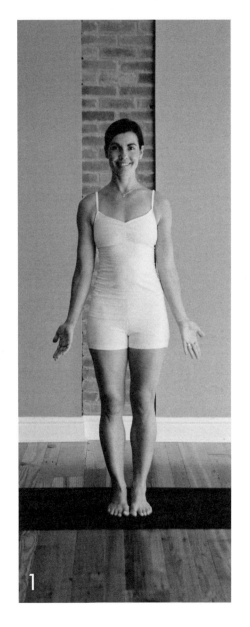

2. Forward Fold (Uttanasana)

(OOT-tan-AHS-ahna); *ut* = intense, *tan* = stretch

Forward Fold is the mother of Rag Doll. This pose naturally lengthens the spine and produces a feeling of relaxation. Forward Fold increases the flexibility of the lower back and the hamstrings.

TIPS

- Fold from the hips instead of the back
- Fingertips in line with the toes
- Engage the thighs to activate the hamstrings
- Weight comes forward
- Head hangs low and relaxed

Modifications:

Bend your knees

3. Half-Way Lift
(Urdhva Mukha Uttanasana)

(OORD-vah MOO-kah OOT-tan-AHS-ahna
urdhva = upward, *mukha* = facing, *ut* = intense,
tan = stretch

Half-way Lift pose lengthens the muscles of the entire spine, including the neck.

TIPS

- Feet together
- Lengthen your spine
- Press your tail bone back
- Crown of the head extends forward
- Shoulder blades draw down the back

Modifications:

Bend your knees

Hands on the shins

4. High Push-Up or Plank Pose

High Push-Up builds upper body and core strength, lengthening the spine and strengthening the low back muscles. It also prepares the body for more challenging arm balances.

TIPS

- Place your shoulders over your wrists
- Fingers face forward
- Feet hip-width distance apart
- Draw the shoulder blades down your back
- Engage the thighs as you lift them towards the ceiling
- Pull your belly up and in
- Press your heels towards the back of the room

5. Low Push-Up
(Chaturanga Dandasana)

(chaht-tour-ANG-ah don-DAHS-anna)
chaturanga = four limbs, *danda* = staff (referring to the spine)

Low Push-Up brings balance and strength to the muscles of the upper body: triceps, biceps, chest, core, and shoulders. Like High Push-Up, it's a nice preparation pose for arm balances. This is not an easy pose! If your elbows wing out, set your knees on the floor. This way, you can isolate your arms and build strength without risking injury!

TIPS
- Move forward as you lower slowly
- Elbows graze the ribs
- Lower until the arms form a right angle (don't let the shoulders dip below the elbows, see photo)
- Push back into your heels

Modifications:

Place your knees on the floor

6. Upward Facing Dog (Urdhva Mukha Svanasana)

(OORD-vah MOO-kah shvon-AHS-anna)
urdhva mukha = face upward, *svana* = dog

Upward Facing Dog strengthens the entire body and opens the chest. It also helps align the spine and stimulates the kidneys and nervous system.

TIPS

- Keep the shoulders on top of the wrists
- Engage the thighs
- Press the tops of the feet down
- Lift the shins and thighs off of the floor
- Shoulder blades relax down

Modifications:
Cobra

7. Downward Facing Dog

WARM-UP SEQUENCE #2 (SUN SALUTATION B)

For the second warm-up sequence we add two new poses: Utkatasana and Warrior 1. Practiced regularly, this warm-up sequence will improve your flexibility, core strength, and cardiovascular fitness level.

1. *Utkatasana*
2. *Forward Fold*
3. *Half-way Lift*
4. *High Push-up*
5. *Low Push-up*
6. *Upward Facing Dog*
7. *Downward Facing Dog*
8. *Warrior 1* (Right foot forward) (Hold for five breaths)

TRANSITIONAL VINYASA

High Push-up
Low Push - up
Updog
Downdog
Warrior 1 (Left foot forward) (Hold for five breaths)

TRANSITIONAL VINYASA

High Push-up
Low Push - up
Updog
Downdog

Repeat three times

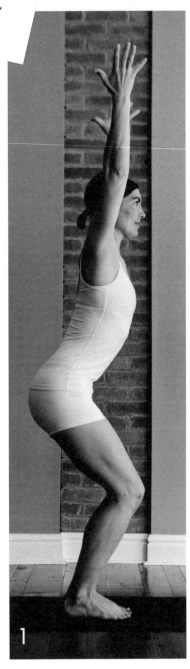

1. Utkatasana

(OOT-kah-TAHS-anna); *utkata* = powerful

Utkatasana strengthens the thighs and the knees, creating strength, balance and stability. It stimulates both the front and back of the thighs, and strengthens the back muscles. It tones and chisels the arms and shoulders.

TIPS

- Straighten your arms
- Rotate the little fingers in and the thumbs out
- Stay firm in your heels, yet light in the toes

Modifications

Don't bend the knees so deep

2. Forward Fold

3. Half-way Lift

4. High Push-up

5. Low Push-up

6. Upward Facing Dog

7. Downward Facing Dog

8. Warrior 1 (Virabhadrasana I)

(veer-ah-bah-DRAHS-anna)

Warrior 1 builds internal heat, strengthening both legs, especially the muscles around the knee. Be a strong and stable warrior: a warrior, not a worrier.

TIPS

- Heels are in one line (heel to heel)
- Back foot is flat at about 45 degrees
- Focus on your back leg: keep it straight and strong!
- Bring the front knee over the ankle
- Press down on the outer edge of the back foot and lift the inner arch up
- Straighten the arms, shoulder blades drawing down your back

SEAN'S POWER SEQUENCE

Warning: This sequence is legal in only 12 states. Before practicing, make sure your state is one of them.

1. Downward Facing Dog

2. Warrior 1 (Right foot forward)

3. Warrior 2 (Hold for five breaths)

4. Extended Side Angle (Hold for five breaths)

5. Reverse Warrior (Hold for five breaths)

6. Triangle (Hold for five breaths

7. Half Moon (Hold for five breaths)

8. Ragdoll (Hold for five breaths)

Transition:

> Release the arms, bring the feet together, reach the arms to the sky, come into Mountain Pose

TRANSITIONAL VINYASA

Repeat side two

1. Downward Facing Dog

2. Warrior 1

3. Warrior 2 (Virabhadrasana II)

(veer-ah-bah-DRAHS-anna)

Like Warrior 1, this pose strengthens both legs and increases stamina. It also strengthens and stretches the chest and shoulders.

TIPS

- Front heel in line with the inner arch of your back foot
- Press the outer edge of your back foot down
- Front knee over the front ankle (stay strong in the back leg!)
- Front knee moves towards the baby toe
- Front thigh parallel to the floor (if possible)
- Spine is perpendicular to the floor
- Engage the arms
- Relax the shoulder blades

4. Extended Side Angle (Utthita Parsvakonasana)

(oo-TEE-tah parsh-vah-cone-AHS-anna)
utthita = extended , *parsva* = side, *kona* = angle

This pose engages all the muscles in the body! Extended Side Angle stretches the side of the body, energizes and strengthens the legs, and stimulates the internal organs. It builds stamina and power.

TIPS

- Press the back foot flat
- Bring the front knee over the front ankle
- Press your feet down and lift your chest up
- Gently press your lower arm into your knee

Modifications:

Place forearm on thigh

5. Reverse Warrior
(Viparita Virabhadrasana II)

(vip-par-ee-tah veer-ah-bah-DRAHS-ah-na)
viparita = reversed or inverted

Increases the flexibility and strength of the legs, back and spine. Stretches the side of the waist and opens the ribs.

TIPS

- Bring the front knee over the front ankle
- Think more about reaching up than stretching back
- Gaze at your fingertips
- Keep your forehead higher than your chin

6. Triangle
(Utthita Trikonasana)

(oo-TEE-tah trik-cone-AHS-ah-na)
utthita = extended, *trikona* = three angle or triangle

Triangle stretches the legs and the muscles around the knee. It works the hips, groin, abdominal muscles, spine, shoulders, and chest. As if that weren't enough, Triangle also stimulates the function of your internal organs.

TIPS

- Straighten the front leg
- Create "space in your waist" (you can always slide your lower hand up onto your shin or a block)
- Keep your torso over your front leg
- Stack the shoulders
- Keep the legs active

Modifications:

Place your hand on your shin or use a block placed outside of your shin.

7. Half Moon (Ardha Chandrasana)

(Say Hello to Your Ass Cheeks Asana)

(ar-dauh chan-DRAWS-ah-na)
ardha = half, *chandra* = moon or luminous

By balancing on one leg at a time, Half Moon strengthens the legs and ankles, the hip abductors, belly and butt. This pose is great for creating balance, focus and coordination. It stretches the hamstrings, calf muscles, shoulders, groin, chest, and spine. Half Moon is a pose in which we practice being okay with falling. It is also known as a mood elevator and is very empowering. It tones the shoulders and arm muscles.

Modifications:

Use a block

Use the wall to help with balance

TIPS

- Place your hand on the floor underneath your shoulder
- Open upper hip over lower hip
- Upper hand is active and reaching

8. Ragdoll

KAREN'S STRENGTH SEQUENCE

Warning: By practicing this sequence regularly, your ass may become so small that the next time you sit on the toilet, you may fall in. Please use caution!

1. Downward Facing Dog

2. Deep Lunge
A. Arms down the sides—five breaths
B. Arms reaching—hold for five more breaths

3. Crescent (hold for five breaths)

4. Standing Split (hold for five breaths)

5. Ragdoll (hold for five breaths)

6. Thighburnerasana (hold for five breaths)

7. Forward Fold

TRANSITIONAL VINYASA

Repeat side 2

After side 2:
A. Reach the arms to the sky, come into Mountain Pose
B. Transitional Vinyasa
C. End in Downward Facing Dog

1. Downward Facing Dog

2A. Lunge Pose with Airplane Arms

2B. Deep Lunge Pose

This pose creates incredible thigh strength and muscle tone. It tones and lengthens the back and neck muscles.

Modifications:

Place your hands on your front thigh

TIPS

- Bring your front knee over the ankle
- Press the back heel towards the back of the room
- Pull your belly up and in to protect your low back
- Squeeze the back thigh
- Pull the chest forward
- Gaze down to protect your neck
- Breathe!

3. Crescent Pose (Anjeyanasana)

(an-jay-AW-nahs-ah-na)

A great heart-opening pose that develops focus, improves balance, coordination, concentration, and builds stamina. Crescent Pose strengthens the core muscles as well as the legs, arms, and back muscles. It increases flexibility for the hips, chest, shoulders, spine, and inner thigh.

TIPS

- Bring the front knee over the front ankle
- Hips face forward
- Back leg straight and strong
- Press the back heel towards the back of the room
- Pull the belly up and in to protect your spine
- The pelvis is neutral
- Straighten the arms, but relax your shoulder blades

Modifications:

Place your back knee on the floor

4. Standing Split
(Urdhva Prasarita Ekapadasana)

Urdhva = upward, *Prasarita* = extended, *Eka* = one, *Pada* = foot

This pose strengthens the legs, lengthens the hamstrings, and improves balance and coordination.

TIPS

- Pull your belly up and in to protect your back
- Drop your head
- Stay strong in the standing leg
- Be light in the toes on the floor

5. Ragdoll

6. Deepthighburnerasana (Deepthighburnerasana) Chair Pose

deep = deep, *thigh* = hunk of flesh, *burner* = on fire

This dynamic pose strengthens the thighs, calves, hamstrings, arms, glutes, and back muscles.

TIPS

- Press your tailbone back
- Pull the chest out
- Hands parallel
- Pull the belly up and in to protect your low back
- Stay firm in the heels, but light in the toes
- Gaze down
- Relax the muscles in your face
- Breathe!

7. Forward Fold

CORE WORK

TRANSITION

1. Downward Facing Dog

2A. High Push-Up on the Forearms

2B. Baby Cobra

Repeat 2–3 times.
Lie down when done and rest.

TRANSITION (after your brief rest)
Upward Facing Dog or Cobra, then back to
Downward Facing Dog

COOL DOWN—LETTING GO

During the final poses do your best to keep up with your breathing. If you find yourself still pushing, fighting or straining, try to relax and keep your focus on what you are feeling. If there is something you are holding on to—competition, greed, doubt—let it go.

1. Downward Facing Dog

2. Half Pigeon (on the right) (hold for 10 breaths)

3. Double Pigeon (on the right) (hold for 10 breaths)

4. Straddle

5. Butterfly

6. Downward Facing Dog

7. Half Pigeon (on the left) (hold for 10 breaths)

8. Double Pigeon (on the left) (hold for 10 breaths)

Transition: use your hands to help you slowly recline onto your back

9. Happy Baby (hold for five breaths)

10. Final Relaxation (at least five minutes)

1. Downward Facing Dog

2. Half Pigeon
(Eka Pada Rajakapotasana)

(aa-KAH pah-DAH rah-JAH-cop-poh-TAHS-ah-na)
eka = one, *pada* = foot , *raja* = king, *kapota* = pigeon

Half Pigeon strengthens and stretches the muscles of the spine, chest and ribcage. It opens and strengthens the groin and hip joints and can be an intense hip opener. It stimulates the spine and the nerves around the spine. Cool-down poses such as this one are vitally important to health and well-being, far more important than building big biceps or gunning for six-pack abs .

Modifications:

Place a block or towel underneath the lifted butt cheek

TIPS

- Place your knee on the floor next to your wrist
- Front thigh is parallel to the side edge of your mat
- Front shin moves toward being parallel with the top edge of your mat (less so if it bothers your hips or knees)
- Flex your front foot
- Square the hips

3. Double Pigeon or Fire Log (Agnistambhasana)

(ahg-nee-stam-BAHS-ah-na)
agni = fire, *stambha* = post or column

This is a deep hip opener that stretches the outer hips and groin.

TIPS

- Stack the shins
- Thigh on the floor is parallel to the side edge of the mat
- Flex both feet

4 - Seated Straddle (Upavistha Konasana)

(oo-pah-VEESH-tah cone-AHS-ah-na)
upavistha = seated, *kona* = angle

This pose stretches the entire back side of the body while opening the hips.

Modifications:

Bend your knees

Hook your big toes

Sit on a blanket to raise the hips

TIPS

- Keep the spine long
- Gently pull the chest away from the navel

5. Butterfly (Baddha Konasana)

(BAH-dah cone-AHS-ah-na)
baddha = bound , *kona* = angle

Butterfly Pose opens the hips, stretches the groin, inner thighs and ankles.

Modifications

Sit on a blanket to raise your hips

TIPS

- Keep the outside edges of your feet on the floor
- Use your elbows to press gently into your knees
- If you need more, walk your arms forward

6. Downward Facing Dog

7. Half Pigeon (on the left side)

8. Double Pigeon (on the left side)

9. Happy Baby (Ananda Balasana)

(ah-NAN-dah bah-LAHS-ah-na)

Happy Baby pose gently stretches the groin and massages the back. It opens and relaxes the hips, and calms the mind. It battles fatigue and relieves stress.

TIPS

- Grab the inside or outsides of the feet
- Bring the ankles over the knees
- Softly draw the knees towards the floor
- Keep your tailbone and head on the floor

Modifications:

Grab under your thighs

10. Final Relaxation (Savasana)

(shah-VAHS-ah-na)
sava = corpse

Never end a yoga session without this final pose. This resting allows the body to absorb all the new energy that you have given it. Keep your awareness and presence during Final Relaxation. Give yourself at least five minutes of Final Relaxation for every 60 minutes of yoga practice. Let go of all control of the breath, the mind and the body. Allow your body to go deeper into a state of total relaxation. This pose reduces stress and tension.

TIPS

- Let your feet fall out to the side
- Palms face up
- Relax your shoulders
- Close your eyes
- Let go of your Ujjayi breathing—breathe silently and softly
- Stay in this pose for at least five minutes
- When finished, sit up slowly

HOW OFTEN SHOULD I DO YOGA?

Every day if possible, even if it's just for 20 minutes. Your body, mind and soul will thank you. Even on days you don't feel up to it, roll out your mat and do a handful of poses. You'll be amazed at the difference it makes in your attitude, how you take on the day with a fresh outlook.

YOGA FOR ATHLETES

When we exercise, we have a finite goal in mind. For instance, when I was training to be an NFL athlete, I wanted to squat 300 pounds. Eventually, I accomplished that. I wanted to kick a football over 70 yards. I trained until I could do that too. But all at a price: my body, degenerated hip flexors and years of incapacitating back spasms. When we train or exercise, we can easily damage our bodies. Yoga can brings us back into balance.

Say you are a top-notch athlete. You have strong muscles, but you likely also have injuries and lack flexibility in certain areas. When we work with the Pittsburgh Steelers, we witness imbalances like these. The players possess incredible strength, but they struggle to touch their toes or turn their neck in one direction. But after a few yoga practices, their bodies begin to open up and they experience release.

Many people turn to yoga after beating up their bodies. They crave physical challenge, yet they are tired of hurting. Yoga is incredible because it is so balanced! It works your muscles, your mind and your heart. Runners love yoga because it heals and strengthens their bodies and here's the magic kicker—it increases lung capacity too.

MEDITATION

A student once asked us, "Do you have any meditation classes?"

"Yes," we said, "All of our classes are meditation classes." Certainly, seated meditation is beneficial and an important practice to bring into your life. But as we have found, and as the yogis of old knew, starting with asana (or poses) calms the mind. We call it a "moving meditation." In fact, you will find that your yoga practice makes it easier to add seated meditation later.

This moving meditation has unbelievable benefits. By holding challenging poses, you learn to remain calm in difficult, even stressful situations. What could be more practical? The next time someone "steals" your parking spot at the grocery store, how will you react? Because you have been practicing being peaceful and calm in stressful situations, you'll be more likely to respond in a nonvolatile way. Moving meditation is something we take off our mats and into our daily lives. We become mindful in every encounter and moment in life, approaching our lives with peace and calmness. We can practice yoga and meditation all day, every day.

THE DISTRACTED MEDITATION STUDENT

A student went to his meditation teacher and said, "My meditation is horrible! I feel so distracted, or my legs ache, or I'm constantly falling asleep. It's just horrible!"

"It will pass," the teacher said matter-of-factly.

A week later, the student came back to his teacher. "My meditation is wonderful! I feel so aware, so peaceful, so alive! It's just wonderful!"

"It will pass," the teacher replied matter-of-factly.

Four

Mindful Eating

AMAZING yoga

Mindful Eating is straightforward, tasty, environmentally conscious, and practical. However, it does require effort and commitment: a commitment to take the time to find out where your food comes from and in some cases, change the way you eat. The suggestions and steps are simple, but be patient and allow the changes in your current eating habits to take place over time. Based on moderation and simplicity, mindful eating takes into account the environmental and economic impact of our dietary choices. Food production should benefit workers, people, and the planet. By taking a moment to see where your food comes from, you can make sustainable and environmentally responsible choices that leave the world better than when you found it. By eating foods that are fresh and close to their natural source, you will feel better, look better, and have more energy. And the closer the better. The average meal travels 1,500 miles to reach your plate!

Most foods on the market are designed to stay on the shelves for a long time. Many contain pesticides, artificial ingredients, hormones, antibiotics, etc., and many are genetically modified. Animals raised on factory farms and kept in confined spaces are fed antibiotics and other artificial drugs. Mother Earth benefits dramatically from sustainable and organic farming. We benefit from eating foods produced locally, organically, and humanely. We have the ability to facilitate change in how our foods our grown, processed, and delivered to us. Every time we visit the grocery store we vote at the check out lane.

We have witnessed the impact of eating locally grown foods at our teacher trainings in Costa Rica and Mexico. We eat just three healthy meals each day—delicious grains, vegetables, and plenty of fruit. Most of the food comes from nearby farms. Snacks are minimal: herbal teas, juices, and fruit. Bodies change dramatically in just one week as people are introduced to natural, nutrient-dense foods. It is a week of detoxification and cleansing. It is also a week where we wake up to the fact that we don't need so much food! During this week we begin to break the "overeating" habit to which many of us are addicted.

It is easy to eat healthily at a yoga retreat. However, eating at home with all the distractions is a different story. With four kids and full schedules it has never been easy, but we fill our house with as many organic fruits, vegetables, and whole grains as possible. We also eat moderate amounts of meats and dairy from organic farmers.

Think of mindful eating as a lifestyle, not a diet. The idea is to eat moderate amounts of whole foods, making sure we get enough protein, fiber, vitamins, minerals, and antioxidants. You will end up eating in a balanced way! As many of us know, fad diets set people up to fail because they aren't sustainable. Once we stop following the rigid rules, once we give into a craving for whatever it is we haven't "allowed" ourselves to eat, our weight rebounds. Mindful eating is not about starving or depriving ourselves so that we can look like a beanpole. It isn't about strict guidelines or counting calories. It's about focusing on being present and enjoying every delicious bite of food. Mindful eating isn't a diet at all, but a decision to make healthy, balanced choices about food and the planet. This is a long-term decision!

We know that each one of us is highly unique. Simply choose what works for you and if it doesn't fit that's ok. This is not meant to be a "one size fits all" eating strategy. Keep in mind that we change as we age, so keep an open mind as we celebrate getting older and wiser.

Eight Mindful Eating Steps to Change Your Life and the World

1. ELIMINATE FAKE FOODS—READ LABELS!

Believe it or not, 90% of the foods Americans consume are processed! Take a look in your cupboards and you'll likely see all sorts of additives: fake fats and sugars, colorings, salt, fake flavors, preservatives, and the list goes on. And what do the food manufacturers take away? The nutrients nature intended for us, like fiber, good fats, and antioxidants. Fortunately, many of these artificial foods are losing popularity as our demand for natural foods grows. Get in the habit of reading labels. If it is not natural, put it back on the shelf.

Avoid the killer duo:

High fructose corn syrup. YUCK! Plentiful because it's cheap, high fructose corn syrup (aliases include "corn syrup" and "corn sweetener") mixes easily, and is very sweet. Research has proven it damages our bodies in many ways, yet the average American consumes 63 pounds of it per year! You'll find high fructose corn syrup everywhere: drinks, sweets, breads (even whole wheat!), frozen foods, beer, spaghetti sauce, and ketchup. Be sure your local schools do not have soda machines.

Partially-hydrogenated fats, also called trans fats. These increase bad cholesterol and decrease good cholesterol, and they cause inflammation. When you cook, use olive oil.

Replace white products with whole grains:

Many bread makers advertise their bread as whole wheat, seven grain, or rye, but check the ingredients! The flour may still be refined and unnecessary sugars are often added. The first ingredients listed should be whole wheat or another whole grain.

2. STAY AWAY FROM REFINED SUGAR

Avoid any food that has added refined sugar. (Soft drinks, cookies, fruit drinks, etc). Refined sugar (white or brown) contains zero nutrients: the only thing it does is elevate your blood sugar levels. White sugar also includes a number of nasty chemicals like phosphoric acid, sulfur dioxide, and formic acid. Those don't sound so good. Avoid artificial sweeteners too: Aspartame, Sucralose *aka* "Splenda," and Saccharin. Too many question marks to list in this book. Eliminate them.

Stick with natural sugars: unrefined raw sugar contains trace minerals and nutrients: calcium, magnesium, iron, phosphorus, and potassium. You can bake with it and it tastes just as good, maybe even better than the refined stuff. Honey is also a good choice in moderation.

3. EAT LESS AND ENJOY MORE!

Most of us eat way too much, too often. A couple of fistfuls is plenty of food. Slow down and chew your food thoroughly. This aids digestions and allows the signal to reach your brain that you are full. The brain needs approximately 20 minutes to know that it is not hungry anymore. Stop eating when you feel satisfied, not when you are full. Stick with just three meals a day. If you need to snack, choose foods such as fruits, veggies, nuts, herbal teas, and natural smoothies.

If we can avoid overeating, we can increase our energy levels, increase our life spans, and experience higher levels of focus. Keeping our body weight at a healthy level minimizes our risks for serious diseases. We can decrease our chances of heart disease, diabetes, and reduce the levels of toxins in our bodies.

When we overeat, it is typically because of boredom, stress, addiction, habit, or unhappiness. We use food to comfort us emotionally or to get through difficult moments. It's hard work to overcome this, so give it time. Be patient as you make changes to your eating habits: your yoga practice will help. Yoga helps us feel better about ourselves. The relaxation we discover through yoga rids us of unneeded attachments and emotions. Instead of stuffing down our emotions with food, we release feelings of greed, anger, resentment, etc. on the mat. Our attitudes lift, our minds become clear and present, and we find ourselves making better decisions about what we eat how much. We stop eating foods that we know are not good for us. As the yoga slows us down and helps us connect, we release ourselves from destructive habits.

4. EMBRACE FRUITS AND VEGGIES!

Replace junk food with fruits and veggies. Why? Because eating fruits and vegetables can:

- Reduce your risk of heart disease and stroke
- Lower your blood pressure
- Reduce your risk of some cancers
- Lower your risk of digestive problems
- Keep your appetite in check

Set a goal of ten servings per day (most of us consume just three), making fruits and vegetables at least 50% of every meal. Include a variety of colors: dark leafy greens and rich yellows, oranges, and reds. Experiment. Keep an open mind and try a new variety each time you to the store or farmers' market. Keep a fruit and veggie bowl available—set it on the kitchen counter.

5. SUPPORT YOUR LOCAL FARMERS!

Buy food from farmers in your area. Many people today are taking part in Community Supported Agriculture, supporting local farmers who deliver fresh foods to your neighborhood. Cooking with what's in season, you will be exposed to fruits and vegetables you won't find at the grocery store, opening you to new recipes and ways to cook. With so many choices, kids actually try new veggies, getting an early start on eating healthy. Eating locally also helps you establish a closer relationship with your farmer and your food as you learn how what you eat is grown. And food fresh from the farm tastes better!

Choose farmers who ensure that their animals and the land are well-treated. Make sure that their products are exceptionally high in nutrition and free of antibiotics and added hormones. Be sure that your meat and dairy products come from grass-fed animals. Local farmers are a great way to obtain grass- fed meat and dairy products, and it's easy to find farmers' markets on the weekends. And speaking of locally, don't forget about your local food banks. Make the effort to give anything extra as often as you can.

Be a farmer yourself. Start your own garden and grow what you love! If you live in a city, search for a community garden.

6. EAT AT HOME. MAKE PREPARING MEALS A CELEBRATION!

Pick up a cookbook or two and experiment with new recipes. Avoid eating out more than once each week. Get family members involved: give kids a role in the process. At one of the places where we hold teacher trainings in Costa Rica the food is incredible. We once asked the cooks how they made an especially wonderful meal and their response was: "Hacemos todo con amor!" "We make everything with love!

7. HAVE A PLAN WHEN YOU GO GROCERY SHOPPING.

Make a list of healthy foods. We have all gone to the grocery store hungry and filled our carts with junk. By sticking to your list, you minimize unnecessary, and often unhealthy, purchases.

Below, you'll find a great shopping list to consider. Keep in mind that there are number of natural foods missing: these are simply the ones we enjoy. Many of these fruits and vegetables were introduced to us by our local farmers—we are so grateful they exposed us to new, healthy foods!

As much as possible, these foods are:

Whole foods, loaded in nutrients

Seasonally available

Affordable

Tasty

VEGGIES
Asparagus
Avocados
Beets
Bok Choy
Broccoli
Brussels sprouts
Cabbage
Carrots
Cauliflower
Celery
Chard
Corn
Cucumbers
Eggplant
Fennel
Garlic
Green beans
Green peas
Kale
Olives
Onions
Potatoes
Romaine lettuce
Spinach
Squash
Sweet potatoes
Swiss chard
Tomatoes
Yams

FRUITS
Apples
Apricots
Bananas
Blueberries
Cantaloupe
Cranberries
Figs
Grapefruit
Grapes
Kiwi
Lemons
Limes
Oranges
Papaya
Pears
Pineapple
Plums
Prunes
Raisins
Raspberries
Strawberries
Watermelon

BEANS & LEGUMES
Great source of fiber, high in protein, and contain folic acid
Black beans
Garbanzo beans (chickpeas)
Lentils
Soybeans
Tofu

RAW NUTS AND SEEDS
High in fiber, nuts aid digestion. They keep you feeling full and help you avoid snacking on crap.
Almonds
Cashews
Peanuts
Walnuts

GRAINS
Brown rice
Oats
Quinoa
Rye Bread
Whole wheat bread

OTHER
Olive oil, extra virgin
Yogurt
Highly versatile, you can mix it with fruit, granola, and honey, or with herbs to make a dip. Use it for fruit smoothies or freeze it to make a delicious snack.
Herbal teas
Perfect with your evening fruit snack.

8. DRINK WATER

Water is our body's #1 nutritional need, and we lose it fast as our body cools, exhales, and eliminates waste. Water helps the body flush out toxins, keeps our skin and heart healthy, and helps us lose weight. Not only is water a healthy alternative to sugary drinks, but it aids digestion and moderates our appetite too. Even mild dehydration can cause headaches and lower our energy levels, and some studies have shown that water even reduces the risk for certain cancers. Invest in a stainless steel water bottle and take it everywhere you go. Invest in a water filter for your home faucet.

Five

Making Everything in Your Life Yoga

AMAZING yoga

When it comes to commitment, most of us are a bunch of "Yes, buts!" YES, we would like to be committed to something, BUT we can't right now, because…

YES, I want to try yoga, BUT I don't have the time.

YES, I know I should pray and meditate more, BUT I'm too tired at night.

YES, I know I could give more time and money to that charity, BUT I want that new car.

The list goes on and on. Yet when we decide something is important to us, we can devote immense time and energy to it.

"What is the difference between people who make a difference in the world and people who choose not to?" a sage once asked. "Are they any smarter, have superior upbringings? Are they better educated, older, younger, black, white, male, female? The answer," he continued, "is none of the above. The answer is the ability to make a commitment, make a promise, and take action."

Now is the time for us to dedicate ourselves to what is important, to something greater than ourselves. Not sports, not becoming famous or making loads of money, not spending our time in other people's business. We have an opportunity to impact people in a positive way, a profound way. Believe in yourself. It's not what we get in life that makes us happy but touching the lives of others that brings us joy. If you want to be happy, try making other people happy.

Karma Yoga, the yoga of daily life, is living as if our actions make a difference, believing that our habits can effect real change. As the Prophet Mohammed said, "God does not judge you according to your bodies and appearances, but He looks into your hearts and observes your deeds." In the scientific terms, this is the law of cause and effect—"What goes around, comes around." Practicing Karma Yoga, we realize that we are here on this planet not to get, but to give, and we do so without seeking recognition or reward, what the yogis call "selfless service."

> In the end, it's not the years in your life that count, it's the life in your years.
>
> ABRAHAM LINCOLN

> If you knew what I know about the power of giving, you would not let a single meal pass without sharing it in some way.
>
> BUDDHA

The Creator gathered the animals and said, "I want to hide something from the humans until they are ready for it. It is the realization that they create their own reality." The eagle said, "Give it to me, I will take it to the moon." The Creator said, "No, one day they will go there and find it." The salmon said, "I will bury it on the bottom of the ocean." "No, they will go there too." The buffalo said, "I will bury it on the Great Plains." The Creator said "They will cut into the skin of the Earth and find it even there." Grandmother Mole, who lives in the breast of Mother Earth, and who has no physical eyes but sees with spiritual eyes, said, "Put it inside of them." And the Creator said, "It is done."

So how do we practice Karma Yoga? You don't need money, you don't need to be a spiritual leader, a guru, a politician, or a priest. No one has a monopoly on doing good deeds. We begin by deciding to be happy. Then, we share that happiness with others. The benefis of yoga appear immediately. Physically, our bodies feel lighter, injuries heal, and our attitudes change. As we strengthen our bodies, we draw on that strength to be of service, to do good. We clean out our attics, de-clutter our minds. As we listen to our bodies instead of our egos, we clean up our thinking, de-clutter our minds. Learning to forgive ourselves, we more easily forgive others. Practicing self-love, we discover we have more love to give. Letting go of anger, greed, jealousy and resentment, we find that making other people happy makes us happy. We move closer to peace.

All we need is a willingness to be kind, to help others—family, friends, neighbors, co-workers, even strangers. This may mean putting ourselves and our desires to the side, but even small gestures go a long way—sending a card, telling your family you love them, listening to someone who needs to tell their story. And never underestimate the value of an encouraging word.

> Service to others is the rent you pay for your room here on earth.
>
> **SHIRLEY CHISHOLM**

So let's dedicate ourselves to what matters: not sports, not becoming famous, not making loads of money, not spending our time in other people's business. It's time to commit to something greater than ourselves. When you encounter negative thoughts, draw on your inner strength and resist the impulse to react with anger. Turn the other cheek. We have an opportunity to impact people in a positive way, a profound way.

Of course, none of us are "there yet." Stay committed to your yoga practice; stay determined on the path of growth. Yoga is a long process, a life-long, spiritual process. Written many years ago, on the tomb of an Anglican Bishop in the crypt at Westminster Abbey, you'll find these words:

When I was young and free and my imagination had no limits, I dreamed of changing the world. As I grew older and wiser I realized the world would not change, and I decided to shorten my sights somewhat and change only my country. But it too seemed immovable. As I entered my twilight years, in one last desperate attempt, I sought to change only my family, those closest to me, but alas they would have none of it. And now here I lie on my deathbed and realize (perhaps for the first time) that if only I'd changed myself first, then by example I may have influenced my family and with their encouragement and support may have bettered my country, and who knows, I may have changed the world.

I can live for two months on a good compliment.

MARK TWAIN

Gentleness, self-sacrifice, and generosity are the exclusive possession of no one race or religion.

GANDHI